The Identity Society

The Identity Society

Revised Edition

William Glasser, M.D.

HARPER & ROW, PUBLISHERS
New York, Evanston, San Francisco, London
1817

The letter to the Los Angeles *Times* from John Severnson Watson, appearing on pages 211-212, is used by permission of Mr. Watson.

The article about Lieutenant Calley, appearing on page 215, is also from the Los Angeles *Times.* Copyright, 1971, Los Angeles Times. Reprinted by permission.

Library of Congress Cataloging in Publication Data

Glasser, William, 1925–
  The identity society.
  Includes index.
  1. Social role. 2. Identity (Psychology)
3. Social values. 4. Social history—1945–
I. Title.
HM101.G55 1975   301.24   74–20403
ISBN 0–06–011565–3

---

75 76 77 78 79 10 9 8 7 6 5 4 3 2 1

To Donald O'Donnell

Contents

Acknowledgments

Although we have never met I would like to acknowledge Marshall McLuhan and also Eric Norden, who did the McLuhan interview in the March 1969 issue of *Playboy* magazine. Here McLuhan stated that "the students are searching for a role, not a goal," which provided the impetus to start this book.

Throughout the past three years my staff at the Institute for Reality Therapy and at the Educator Training Center listened, questioned, and used these ideas, to provide me with incentive to continue. All they did and still do is deeply appreciated.

As in my previous books, my cousin Robert Glasser acted as editorial consultant, but much more so in this book than before. I wish it were possible to show the amount of work he did. Each chapter was reworked painstakingly, some as many as ten times, in the more than two years we worked together. He posed well over fifteen hundred rigorous questions that had to be answered or the material deleted. More than ever, I am grateful for his help.

I would like to thank the Honorable George Dell, Judge of the Los Angeles County Superior Court, who took time from his pressing schedule to review the legal material in Chapter Nine.

It hardly seems possible, now when the book is done, that so much typing was needed along the way. Some chapters were typed more than twenty times, all at least ten times, as the book progressed. Most was done by Beverly Rumbles, but a great deal by Nancy Hollingsworth, Eileen Wolfe, and Laurel Jacoby. Final copyediting was also done by Robert Glasser, but a fine job of preliminary copyediting was con tributed by Harriette Berkely. Thanks also to my editor at Harper & Row, Harold Grove, who encouraged me from the start to finish.

WILLIAM GLASSER

Los Angeles
October 1975

The Identity Society

Evidence of Change

The chain of events that led to the idea of the identity society started in 1965 when I began to work in the Los Angeles public schools, initially in the inner city near Watts. There, the difficulty in motivating students to do traditional school work alerted me to the drastic changes occurring in our society, changes that were affecting both students and teachers. This book, however, is not about the schools. They are mentioned here only because they so clearly reflect what is occurring not only to students but to all of us—the half-billion people who live in the affluent Western world—who are moving right now into what I believe is best called an *identity society*.

Once the idea of the identity society came I could see that what I was encountering in the schools applied in many other situations. I came to believe that the failure of prisons, reform schools, and mental hospitals, the failure of many marriages and the resultant family problems, and the growing number of individuals who are unhappy with their lives but do not know clearly why are all part of an emerging pattern that is all around yet difficult to see.

As I was searching for this pattern I read an interview with Marshall McLuhan in the March 1969 *Playboy* magazine. McLuhan's reply to a question about social unrest seemed to provide the answer I was seeking. He said, "From Tokyo to Paris to Columbia, youth mindlessly acts its identity quest in the theatre of the streets searching not for *goals* but for *roles*, striving for an identity that eludes them."

McLuhan explains that the students are searching for a role, an identity reached only through personal fulfillment. Throughout history most people have thought little about attaining an identity because it was beyond their grasp. They were content to reach a goal, minimally to survive, hopefully to become secure. McLuhan believes that recently something new has happened, that while the traditional struggle for a goal—a job, a diploma, a home, a secure family—still exists, now suddenly it has been preceded by the struggle to find oneself as a human being, to become aware of and enjoy the pleasures implicit in our own humanity. Unlike the traditional goals, which may vary widely, role, or, as I prefer to call it, our new desire for identity, is about the same for all people. Today almost everyone aspires to live in a way that can provide a happy, successful, pleasurable belief in himself. Role, or identity, is now so important for the young that it must be achieved in some degree before they will work hard for any goal. As a society we can no longer afford to ignore this new priority in human motivation. For example, institutions such as schools and families that function as if this new motivational sequence did not exist are now in serious trouble.

It is my argument that today almost everyone is personally engaged in a search for acceptance as a person or as a person performing a task rather than as a performer of a task alone. Blacks may search for identity through black power, women through women's liberation and consciousness-raising sessions, and businessmen through meditation. Even the armed forces, a most unlikely institution to recognize personal identity, are beginning to do so. They are adopting new training and living procedures in which the recruit is to some degree accepted as a human being, not just as a body to serve without question.

Tradition, however, has far from run its course. Institutions of our society, especially our schools, still operate with insufficient humanity, that is, as if goal took precedence over role. They are slowly changing, however. The demonstrations and occasional violence on our campuses, provoked by our intellectual youth, that called our attention to the change toward an identity society have run their course. The ending of demonstrations is due partly to a change in the colleges toward a more human approach to students and partly to the withdrawal of American troops from Southeast Asia. In our high schools, there is apathy and increased use of drugs, and of alcohol. Nevertheless, as our society has responded generally to the ending of demonstrations with more acceptance of our young, there are many indications that at least the intellectual young are responding with hard work and the pursuit of goals. We, however, should not be misled by a new soberness of one segment of our young into thinking that the clock has turned back. It never has and never will. We will see more of the response we are seeing—a pursuit of goals—if we can give all of our young the personal support and the recognition that they need and deserve but that most of them do not now get. Given adequate recognition, however, at home and at school, many more young people will direct their energy into pursuing a goal because they know that a role—an identity that is fulfilling—is not gained through passive involvement with personal pleasure. More will discover that it has to be tied to work and accomplishment, that happiness must be thoughtfully and vigorously pursued or it disappears.

In the seventies we are seeing the blue collar young join the search for an identity as the college students did in the sixties. Studs Terkel, in his 1973 book *Working*, describes the shift toward the search for personal fulfillment not only in the blue-collar young but in the lives of workers of all ages and occupations. As they tell their stories in his book, the different people show a constant preoccupation with the human parts of their lives and how they wish to fulfill themselves more regardless of what they do. There is anger, suffering, and apathy among many who find their lives dull and unrewarding. If ever a book were written to support the concept of the identity society, *Working* is (inadvertently) that book.

As we move into the identity society, almost everyone is secure enough (or thinks he may soon be) so that the old motivations of security and fear are being challenged by the new motivation of personal fulfillment. Although unemployment and inflation may reduce security and cause these motivations again to come into conflict, it is the thesis of this book that we have entered a new epoch. Five hundred million people have had enough of a taste of fulfillment, or at least realize that they are missing something important, so that they will not return to or accept the personally dehumanizing way of life that too many have accepted for too long.

Note: See Appendix for a speculative anthropological explanation of where this new identity society fits into the five-million-year history of mankind.

Chapter One

The Identity Society

Led by the young, the half-billion people of the Western world have begun a rapid, turmoil-filled evolution toward a new role-dominated society that I call the identity society. Less anxious than formerly about fulfilling goals to obtain security within the power hierarchy, people today concern themselves more and more with an independent role—their identity. Of course, people still strive for goals; increasingly, however, they are goals, vocational or avocational, that people believe will reinforce their concept of themselves as persons. For example, not everyone can work at a job that gives him a lot of satisfaction such as that of doctor, artist, or teacher, but anyone can pursue a recreational goal, such as bowling or playing bridge, or a volunteer goal, such as working in a hospital or fund raising, that reinforces his view of himself as someone.

In the countries that have moved into the new identity society, there is now suddenly enough security so that personal fulfillment *seems* possible for almost everyone. It is not whether it is possible but that it seems possible that has led almost everyone to overcome the traditional survival fears and look for happiness. Rather than work for a goal and then search for personal satisfaction, young people today strive first for a fulfilling role, for something to do that has personal significance and promises pleasure. They may then work hard for a goal that can establish this role. A young doctor's view of himself in the new identity society illustrates this change:

> I am a doctor not because I can make money and find a very secure, prestigious place for myself high in the power structure but because I think I can practice medicine to become involved with my fellow man. I'd like to work in an inner city hospital, in the Peace Corps, in a "free" clinic, in research, or for the Public Health Service. I expect to get paid enough to live, perhaps to be comfortable; but to me being a doctor is much less to gain money, prestige, and power than it is to reinforce my own role, my belief in myself as a human being. As I struggle helping others, I will enjoy the satisfaction that comes when I do this well.

The dean of my medical school has remarked that students who before 1950 answered the standard question, "Why do you want to become a doctor?" with "For the pleasure of working with people" (the role answer) were often refused admission, suspect as some kind of a nut or troublemaker; the student who answered that he wanted a secure profession (the goal answer) was accepted. Since about 1950, Western Reserve University Medical School, for one, has been admitting many students who say they are interested in public service.

Today, everyone tries to use work, service, or play to gain a successful identity through involvement with others and through goals that help him to be successfully involved. Many people fail, however, in the difficult task of achieving a successful identity. Unable to do so, to do something with their lives that gives them fulfillment, but still desperate to be somebody, they settle for a failure identity: emotional disturbance, antisocial behavior, crazy thinking, or sickness—all attempts to reduce the pain of their failure.

An analogy may help explain the new identity society. Many people find that it is like going to a party when there is plenty of food but you are not hungry. You try to make contact with some of the other guests but no one is interested in you. You cannot leave because you came with someone who is having a good time and who does not want to leave. As the evening goes on and you cannot get into a good conversation, you begin to get anxious. You are in a painful situation. Although you believed you had no serious social problems, the evening was a nightmare of rejection. You were willing to give of yourself to others but there were no takers. No loneliness is more acute than the loneliness that exists in a crowd where most of the people are obviously enjoying each other's company.

What happened to you at the party represents failure in the identity society. You already have security; now you need frequently to be verified as a person by your fellow man. When you do not get the involvement that gives you this verification, you suffer. You want the people, not the food, because the only way you can maintain a successful identity is to accept and be accepted by others whom you respect and who believe you are worthwhile. A successful identity, therefore, is gained through involvement, not through a full stomach. But because no one can demand involvement, it is easier to leave and be alone than to suffer. Being alone may be temporarily less painful, but in the end if you stay alone because you fear rejection you suffer as much or more. This suffering is important to understand; it is explained in the two following chapters.

A married woman who works further illustrates the change from emphasis on survival to emphasis on identity. Does she work because she needs people or because she needs money? And if she needs money, is it for survival or to give her a better way of life? Would she continue to work if her husband got a large raise? Suppose she is a young school teacher about to marry a wealthy young man. For several years she was careful to succeed as a school teacher. Following the principal's lead she stayed close to the curriculum as well as to the written rules. Because she had little security, she needed her job and the praise possible from doing a good job. Praise from the principal gave her security but now she no longer needs her job for security. After marriage she and her husband decide that she will continue to teach school. Now the situation is different. She teaches because she enjoys the children, because she has friends on the faculty, and because she is happy and successful. If the principal criticizes her bulletin boards or her control of the class when the children are a little exuberant, she smiles to let him know that he should not worry. She is here because she wants to be here, not because the job gives her security. She now gently demands to be considered a more independent, less predictable person. Today in the identity society she is usually a better teacher because of her altered role.

An engineer in a large firm that fills government contracts works hard. He is concerned with his status because he considers status a good indication of security. He is interested in the size of his office, the number of men with whom he shares a secretary, the dining room to which he has access, and whether or not he has his name on a parking place. When layoffs start, he makes countless calculations about his position in the layoff hierarchy. If his skill is narrow, he is very insecure and may encourage his wife to work to increase the family security. If pushed too far, with a little show of independence, he will defend himself as a human being with human rights; always fearful of the boss, however, he worries when he does so. Gaining an illusion of independence when times were good and government contracts plentiful, he lives up to his income and has changed jobs frequently to get raises.

The engineer was and is goal-oriented, but his children, raised in security, are role-oriented. Like many successful men in their forties and older, he cannot understand why they are so different from him. Yet both he and his wife asked their children to contribute much less to the family security than their parents asked of them. They encouraged their children to achieve their own potential and enjoyed seeing them do so. But because they wanted their children to work toward a security profession, the parents fretted when they did not quickly start to do so.

Their attitude caused their children to think more about themselves (as many people did in the new and comparatively affluent society that followed World War II). Valuing themselves, the children cared less about goals than their parents had. They were concerned, rather, with their role, with their human potential, and with their happiness. No longer squelched as it had been for 10,000 years, the need for identity revealed itself freely and strongly in the children born since 1940. When they work for a goal, as many do, the goals they work for are those that now or later will reinforce their role.

Once the economically secure child overtly started his search for an independent role by growing a beard or by participating in a peace march or in a voter registration drive or, at a different level, by using drugs or dropping out of school, many parents attempted to deny that the security they gave their child could have led to the present behavior that they deplored. Because the children's behavior is not goal behavior and is thus not acceptable to most older parents, some parents have rejected or even attacked their children, quickly causing a wide gap between parent and child.

Rather than the well-advertised generation gap, this is a cultural gap. Today in many families there are two cultures: the parents, who are goal-oriented, live in one and their children, who are role-oriented, live in the other. Less than thirty years into the new identity society, we find most families with older children to be divided culturally. In the next generation, as the identity society children become parents, the cultural gap should narrow. Although there are some indications that this narrowing is already occurring, much conflict still exists between parents and children. As a result the growing child who strongly expresses his new role may lose the support of his parents, support provided so freely when he was younger. He needs parental involvement more than ever when he is an adolescent and a young adult if he is to achieve a successful role. If he cannot find involvement within his family, he will look outside his family. If he fails to find involvement readily, as he often will, he may give up on human involvement the way the fox gave up on the grapes. Rather than bringing him back to a goal orientation, his parent's rejection only isolates him further, an isolation that leads to failure in the identity society. To make his human failure less painful, he may develop painful physical symptoms and then perhaps turn to drugs to relieve the pain. Those who cannot find involvement today are almost always doomed to failure and misery.

Unlike the cultural gap, a generation gap always existed; although questioning their parents' values was normal for children, rejecting their parents' values was unusual. In earlier times children argued that they wanted to achieve a goal in a different way or that they wanted to try for a new goal foreign to their parents. For example, they may have wanted to leave the farm and seek their fortune in the city. They rarely questioned the traditional sequence of goal before role. A child learned from his parents that hard work was necessary and that he was unrealistic if he thought the world would let him search for fulfillment. A few young people who were secure in their family probably went through a limited struggle attempting to find a fulfilling role before they attained a goal. As soon as they went out into the world away from the security of their home, however, they gave up trying to establish an independent role. Knowing that the children were behaving as they had, or wish they had, behaved when they were young, adults encouraged them with amused toleration in the mild rebellion. Children were allowed their high jinks and their wild oats as long as they did not threaten the established and secure order.

Now it is different. Our present younger generation was raised by an older generation that itself has become secure enough to begin to be concerned about fulfillment. The older generation has moved this far because most of them feel secure; this security, together with increased communication and political enlightenment, has allowed the younger generation to move even further and to assert early their desire for identity. They refuse to put aside this desire just because in the past young people did so. The power structure and the family, both weakened by increased security, are in trouble partly because they attempt to stand in the way of young people as they struggle for a successful role. Because the young have had security and freedom within their family, they believe that an independent role is possible; they do not hear their family's admonition that the security and freedom are temporary because they are provided not by the society but by the family. They hope the government or private enterprise will provide role-reinforcing work. If they are unable to find such work, they struggle to find a successful identity in some other way. Should they fail, as many do, they fight or become apathetic and give up. They then become a burden both to themselves and to society.

The shift to the identity society is not limited to the more publicized young—the hippies, the demonstrators, and the social drop-outs. Although it is not so obvious in other young people, many of whom work hard, it is a rare young person today who is willing to subordinate his identity to security. Almost all are working primarily to support a satisfying concept of themselves. The more successful this concept is, the harder they work. The motivation is positive—gaining a stronger feeling of self, rather than the old negative motivation—the fear of insecurity.

The precedence of role over goal present in most young people today is by no means limited to the young. For example, in the traditional sequence a middle-aged corporate executive adopts the corporate goals, works hard, moves often, and obeys all the rules. He finally gains enough security to refuse a higher-salaried job in a new city because he and his family enjoy the human satisfactions that are part of his present community. In the new society, the young man starting to work for a corporation asks immediately about the potential for human satisfaction on the job. Although he may not always dress, look, or even act the part according to traditional corporate practice, he may work hard to attain the personal, as well as the financial, reward of the job. As he moves up in the company, he may give up superficial non-conformities such as dress style, not because he is afraid or insecure, but because it is easier for him to fight more important battles without wasting his energy on small irritations produced by his nonconformity. Now conforming superficially, he has time and energy for activities both at work and elsewhere that reinforce his independent role.

In the old society a student might never question a professor until he had completed all of his work. Then, with some trepidation, he might question his professor and give his opinion; if the professor listened, the student might begin to achieve a role. He did the work first, however; goal preceded role. Today's student may sometimes (with little knowledge) question his professor immediately. His challenge to the teacher's authority supports his idea of himself as a person even before he has done the work to gain recognition. A patient, tolerant, and attentive professor may motivate this student to work as hard as ever for a goal by listening to him and then pointing out that doing the work will further support his new role. An intolerant or impatient professor may cause the student to lose interest and settle for goals that reinforce failure, not success.

Many older people accept the importance of role. They firmly believe, however, that a role should be achieved through traditional pathways. That is, a person should first work hard to gain security and only then try to attain a role. Older people maintain that everyone should be primarily goal-oriented. They still venerate goals even though, once successful, they no longer spend much time working for them.

The young say that this traditional order is inhuman and degrading. They maintain that our identity is as basic as our humanity and that we should, therefore, reject goals that do not immediately and directly reinforce our basic human role.

Seeing little value in power or property for its own sake, they believe that power, property, and technology should support and reinforce people and their roles as human beings. They should not be so expanded that they prevent people from achieving a role. Young people deny the value of any goal that does not reinforce humanity.

Let us now examine the three primary reasons for the recent, sudden emergence of the identity society. Affluence, one of the three driving forces for change, affects the half-billion people of the Western world. Of the three and a half billion on earth, only these half-billion people are affluent or, equally important, believe they soon may be. In the Western world we have almost entirely eliminated the fear of nonsurvival. The starving are so few that they do not affect the thinking of the society. Also, some poor people make little trouble because, with the loosening of the power hierarchy and with the narcotizing influence of TV, they do not realize they are on the bottom. They are so bombarded with the possibilities of affluence that they gain the illusion that somehow they will soon share in the abundance around them. Even if they think that they are not likely to share in the wealth that they see, they tend to become dissatisfied more as personal failures than as economic failures. Their pain is more social than economic. And even people on the bottom or close to it know that the bottom is better than it was in the past. With more money and more education, young people and all people in the Western world have greater opportunities than ever before. In the United States, the GI Bills, both for education and for housing, exemplify political thinking that led to the affluence that caused the identity society to emerge.

The second important force to lead us into the identity society is political enlightenment for human rights. Freedom has expanded in most of the Western world. Even in countries with less freedom, such as Spain and Korea, the young are protesting and, to some extent, being heard. Although many role-dominated young people think that any infringement on total personal freedom is political oppression, that they can protest so freely and loudly that people all over the world listen to them, partly belies the charge that they have no real freedom.

The protests, however, do threaten the power structure especially when those in power believe that some of the older, more goal-oriented people, upon whom the power structure depends, will listen. Although the protestors usually do not want to become violent, the power structure, in order to reduce the support of older people who abhor violence, sometimes provokes it. As governments begin to understand the implications of the identity society—that human rights cannot be easily put aside—and as protestors discover that violence robs them of much of their support, more progress toward giving people a chance for an independent role will occur.

Because the protests are a manifestation of the cultural gap between the old and young, frustration will sometimes lead to violent demonstrations. As long as the Vietnam war continued, the protests continued because war is incompatible with an independent human role. Although an identity society could fight a war either to defend itself or to extend human freedom, no American soldiers in Vietnam believed that they were fighting for either of these goals. They were fighting only for their own survival. Although some soldiers with a successful identity at times refused to risk their lives, the identity society army did not often court-martial them. Instead the army command talked to them and tried to persuade them to obey orders, using coercion as little as possible because it recognized that on any large scale coercion would not work.

The Vietnam war, the first war fought in part by an identity society and its soldiers, provided daily evidence of the erratic and inconsistent support given it by our government. Little concerned with the professed goals of the country—and many did not know what they were—the soldiers became concerned with the practical goal of making their forced servitude as painless and safe as possible. Although many soldiers took easily available drugs because they felt failure, frustration, and intense fear, few became addicted. When they returned home to a society where they could gain some value, the pain and frustration disappeared. Most were able to give up even large doses of drugs because they no longer had need for them.

In addition to permitting protests, additional examples of political enlightenment are laws and court decisions liberalizing divorce and abortion as well as those protecting civil rights and the rights of accused criminals. Laws guaranteeing individual freedom, if implemented, can provide more people the chance to live successfully in a new society.

The media, especially television, are a final and perhaps most important factor causing the emergence of the identity society. Since the early 1950's most people have grown to depend on television for much of their evening and weekend pleasure. Young children are estimated to watch television more than two thousand hours before they start school. Television has influenced the lives of almost everyone in the Western world. Programs and commercials both tell us constantly that personal worth and personal pleasure are most important. Television tells people that they should be dissatisfied with the status quo, that they can experience more in life than they presently do, that they should be aware of the unlimited possibilities of their own humanity, and, finally, that they can best achieve their own human potential by using the various products advertised or by living like the people shown in the programs.

Although most people did not recognize the advent of the identity society until recently (and some still do not), the advertising world sensed the change shortly after World War II. Not only did advertisers know about it, but they have also, through the media, accelerated and consolidated our rapid shift into the identity society. The earliest ads—handbills, posters, newspapers, and magazines—stressed economy. These goal ads, urging us to buy a product or service because it was the best deal for the money, were directed to thrifty, goal-oriented people. Money meant security; thus the best buy created the most security. Comfort, pleasure, and ease of use were important but secondary to value. Used products and essential products such as simple foods and hardware are still advertised for value. Value was the advertised attraction even with nonutility products such as Pepsi-Cola, with the attention-getting jingle of the 1930's and 1940's "Twelve full ounces, that's a lot" and "Twice as much for a nickel, too." If you were thirsty and wanted a cola drink, for a nickel you could get twice as much Pepsi as you could of Coca-Cola, its leading competitor.

Since the mid-forties totally goal-oriented, price-is-primary advertising has disappeared for many utility products. The goal or utility of the product is now partly subordinated to supporting the role of the buyer. Volkswagen ads, for example, appeal to your ability as a affluent person who could buy a more expensive car to be independent and thoughtful. To encourage a person to buy a VW when he could afford more, they urge him to take on a thrift role and couple it with Volkswagen.

Advertisers recognize that most people over thirty are still concerned with security and must be reached through ads that stress the importance of gaining recognition in what one does. A housewife does not want to be just a housewife; she wants to be the best and most successful housewife in the neighborhood. In successfully performing her dependent role of a good laundress, for example, she is in friendly competition with other housewives. A television commercial shows a woman taking her linens out of a washing machine while an astonished neighbor exclaims, "How did you get your sheets so white?" Bursting with pride, she says, "It's not me at all; it's Axion! It makes my clothes not just white but whiter than white," a claim that few can top. Ads that reinforce pride in the dependent role are tied to almost all utilitarian products. They rarely mention price. "Whiter than white" confirms one's role as a housewife; questioning the price of a product that gives so much dependent role confirmation would be bad taste. Cake mixes, foods, floor waxes, window cleaners, insurance, and other utilitarian or consumable products are often advertised to confirm your role as a good cook, a good housewife, a good home maintenance man or, a prudent homeowner.

Some products are sold almost completely on their advertised ability to get a person involved and help him toward a successful identity. High-utility products such as automobiles might be advertised on their intrinsic value; others of low or adverse utility such as beer, soft drinks, cosmetics, and cigarettes are best sold without any reference to their value. Ads divorcing the product totally from utility and attempting to tie it solely to a person's independent role represent the full flourishing of identity ads. One of the first successful identity society ads was the Pepsi-Cola ad of 1951. When Pepsi-Cola gave up "Twice as much for a nickel, too," and hammered home the message, "Be sociable, drink Pepsi," the identity ad was on its way. The ad implied that Pepsi could provide sociability and involvement; if you were lonely and unfulfilled, Pepsi could help you. With no explanation (obviously there are more sociable drinks around), Pepsi was tied to the need for involvement. In 1969 Pepsi-Cola went further by calling the new society "The Pepsi Generation," the young, fun-loving, involved generation; the identity society was, in essence, the Pepsi Society. Pepsi ads show the way to sell successfully products of little utility in a goal sense but of high utility in an independent role sense.

Identity ads promote an individuality that stresses social or sexual desirability. They state or intimate that without these products you will never achieve the appeal necessary for involvement. Going even further, the Winston ad tells you that, with a Winston cigarette, you will always have a friend. The product is no longer the key to involvement, it is now involvement itself; with a Winston, you need nothing else. It's enough to tempt a lonely nonsmoker to smoke. Few ads go as far as Winston or Pepsi, but they all imply the promise of love and happiness. Although high-fashion, expensive products may briefly mention their utility, a person buying expensive clothes, jewelry, or cars actually buys reinforcement of his identity. Ad agencies that cannot sense how strong the need for involvement is and cannot work it into their ads will not thrive; even rich people, however, like to believe that there is shrewdness and utility in their purchase of a three-hundred-dollar suit. Successful ad agencies need the skill to weave utility and identity together in a subtle appeal to both. For low-utility products such as beer, soft drinks, or cosmetics, however, or for adverse utility products such as cigarettes, no such nonsense is necessary. The product whose ads convince you that the product is the answer to the elusive quest for successful identity will succeed. Products whose ads do not provide this reinforcement fail.

Television programs and movies that do not sufficiently appeal to the audience's need for involvement will also fail the way the lonely Edsel no one needed failed. The old, highly successful "escape" movies that led people briefly to imagine themselves in the independent roles of the wealthy played by Cary Grant or Irene Dunne were appropriate for a culture in which the average man had great difficulty finding escape. Now with our increased security we do not always want to escape. Sometimes we want to face (on the screen) the struggle for human involvement when the going is tough. *On the Waterfront* was an early movie of this kind. Even Westerns are now patterned more after *Shane* than *Hopalong Cassidy*. Some movies, such as *The Graduate, Butch Cassidy and the Sundance Kid*, and *Love Story*, cause both the old and the young to become involved. Others, such as *Easy Rider* and *Midnight Cowboy*, flouting traditional values and exploring the cultural gap, appeal mostly to the young. Even the older generation is losing its traditional goal values and discovering some of these pure role movies.

TV programs such as "All in the Family," the "Mary Tyler Moore Show," and "Sanford and Son" show people behaving in very human ways, not as the expected stereotypes of traditional television pap. Because they do, we identify with them and become personally involved. As most people are now searching for involvement, these programs have had unexpected popularity. Television programs such as "Bonanza," which show family involvement and exemplify good father-son relationships, are also successful. In all these programs the plots resolve happily and the characters have economic security and lead the good life.

Unlike movies, which sometimes show failure and misery, television rarely shows threats to security such as the lonely or starving life, except in occasional dramas or documentaries that may create some brief interest. At long as threatening programs are shown infrequently, people may enjoy them because they can favorably compare their own affluence with the misery on television. Because the viewers do not become involved with the people in the drama or documentary, they are more reinforced than threatened. Occasionally, people do become involved with documentaries. They then may show concern for their fellow man's lonely misery or for their own security which, previously taken for granted, may be threatened. After the documentaries "Hunger in America" and "The Selling of the Pentagon" were presented, people, exhibiting concern for the loneliness and misery of others and for their own lack of security, began to question their government.

Children, who watch a great deal of television and know nothing other than the identity society, get constant reinforcement that they are important, that they are valuable, and that they should lead the good life. Although radio, magazines, and newspapers have influenced and still do influence people, television, because of its nature and because of the time involved, has a greater influence on people, especially the young and impressionable, than any of the other media. Its potentially insidious and destructive influence is discussed in Chapter Five. With its vivid portrayal of a secure nation, television has been a major factor in helping people believe they are secure enough to concern themselves with the need for involvement, a concern required for us to move into the identity society. As long as television exists in its present form, it is doubtful that we will ever go back to the survival society. Television says, "You are important and your role is important. Do everything you can to reinforce your role by identifying with the programs and by using the hairspray, beer, and soft drinks that will help you get involved." That the life shown on television programs is more fantasy than reality, that sociability through Pepsi is more promise than guarantee, or that making money to buy a Mustang is more hard work than pleasure is of no concern to the programmers. If they get the message across that this life, and these products are what you need, they have done their job.

Rock music, listened to almost religiously by almost all young people, reinforces the identity society. Unlike the lyrics of the thirties and early forties, which relied heavily on "June, moon," and "jingle, jangle, jingle" the words of rock music are often serious, describing the desires and frustrations of the young as they attempt to find an identity. The music, emphasizing beat, is also involving. The performers are of course flamboyant examples of individuality. Together, the words, music, and performers have profoundly influenced young people to reinforce their role orientation.

Therefore, there have been three major forces that have come together in strength to cause the new identity society. Affluence or its promise exists for most people in the Western world. Political liberty, at least compared with what we have known in the past, exists for most people in the Western world. Even those at the bottom have some protection against degradation under the political systems of most countries of the West. Finally, we have created role-reinforcing forms of communication that dominate the lives of so many people, especially young people in their formative years. Television must be considered a cornerstone of the identity society.

In the last few years people—common people, poor people, uneducated people, powerless people, as well as the more affluent—are beginning to ask themselves the basic existential questions: "Who am I?" and "What is my human potential?"

If we ask a teenage girl, representative of the young people who seem to illustrate the point most clearly, "What is most important to you?" she usually answers, "To be myself." We ask her, "What do you mean, to be yourself?" She says, "To be me, to enjoy myself, to stand for something, to have my own feeling of being someone, to have friends, to have values, to be accepted by others."

If you ask her and others to explain further, they say that they want to be accepted for their own humanity, as human beings, regardless of what they do, as long as they do not hurt or restrict others. Further, they claim that giving and receiving pleasure and love, which they tie closely together, are basic to their humanity; the highest value is love and the lowest value is premeditated harm to another person. They believe that all human life must be respected and conserved. For human beings to live a human life, they must have as natural an environment as possible; when we disrupt our environment we reduce our human potential.

Work for them is not necessarily sacred. If a man chooses not to work he should have a right not to work. Although most young people want to work, they believe our society should provide more jobs that reinforce the independent role. If you ask, "If a person doesn't work, who will support him?" they say, "His friends." They do not believe a person has a right to prey upon others who do not wish to support him, but they believe no one should be criticized if his friends decide to care for him. They also believe that each person has an obligation to work to increase the quality of life for all and that the obligation includes limiting births.

In discussing the identity society, I have so far stressed involvement which in a broad sense is synonymous with love. Also important is work because it can reinforce the independent role, or it can provide the security for a person to find a role in another way by doing something else that will reinforce his independent role.

Therefore, from talking and working with both young and old people in the new society, I have concluded that two human qualities are necessary to gain a successful identity: love and worth. First, one has to love and be loved—to be involved with people whom one cares for and respects. Second, one must do a worthwhile task that increases his sense of self-worth and usually helps others to do the same. Whether the person is a teacher or a manufacturer who gives others jobs, whether in a hobby or in volunteer work, the task must have a goal that reinforces a sense of worth. Also what one chooses that he believes is worthwhile must, sooner or later, be considered of value by someone else. A person may labor alone as an artist or scientist for years, but eventually what he produces must be recognized by others or he will not gain a successful identity. As security was the key to success in the now-ending survival society, so love and personal worth are the keys to a successful identity in the new identity society.

One characteristic of the identity society that must be specifically mentioned is the open concern for sexual gratification. With this concern has come discussion of sex and some new considerations of what sex means to the individual. For example, the double standard of sexual behavior, in which men could indulge in sex prior to marriage and women could not, has already changed. This and other changes in our attitude toward sex are discussed in Chapter Eight.

Perhaps the most profound effect of the identity society has been the women's liberation movement. Women are demanding that men and women be treated equally. These demands have been so strong that the almost all-male Congress has passed an equal-rights amendment to the Constitution that appears to be on the way to ratification by the states. Women have passed beyond their initial requests for (1) equality of opportunity, (2) equal pay for equal work, (3) the right not to have children, and (4) available child care to free them for other pursuits. Although much has been accomplished on each of these four points, they are far from being fully accepted. In addition, however, women in divorce actions now want financial recognition both for the "intangible" wages they have earned in hard household labor and for their lost earning power when they cut off a career to do housework. They also point out the need to allow them credit and all financial services on the same basis as men. Personally, women want control over their own bodies not only for pregnancy but also for more humane and less male-oriented gynecological examinations. They are demanding that procedures in rape trials be changed so that the victims are no longer subject to indignities almost as bad as the attack. Another demand is that elementary school textbooks and readers be changed to eliminate the strong sexual stereotyping present in almost all current books for the young. As sexual stereotypes are broken down, a by-product of the women's liberation movement will be the liberation of men from their own restrictive stereotypes.

In summary, in our society people are not more concerned about who they are than about security. In this chapter we have shown how vital involvement is to satisfying this concern and to gaining a successful identity. But not all people gain a successful identity, and in the next two chapters we will examine the serious difficulties of those who fail.

Chapter Two

Pleasure and Pain

Pleasure or pain is the basis of most of our behavior. Just as the pain of rejection or loneliness drives some of us to drugs or alcohol, even though we know that making new friends is a better choice, so the pleasure of sex, not the desire for children, causes most of us to make love frequently. As we have evolved over the past four million years from primitive men living in small groups to civilized men living in large societies, our feelings and the actions they cause have become progressively more complex. For modern man, who rarely experiences the extreme pain and fear that must have been common to primitive man, painful, uncomfortable feelings commonly take the form of anxiety, depression, or fatigue. It is difficult to find an obvious cause for these feelings or see clearly how to behave differently to reduce the pain.

The biologic purpose of pain is for survival. It focuses our attention and warns us of danger that requires some response. A little pain tells us to change what we are doing; if we do not, the pain will intensify. Sometimes we respond reflexively,

26

without thinking. When we lean back against a hot stove, we jump forward; no one takes time to think about various alternatives. Often we have time to seek a reasonable response, although without much thinking. If we are out in the sun too long, we look for shade. Most of our responses to pain are more complicated; for example, the pain of sickness urges us to ask someone to care for us. Alone, we would often be overwhelmed by the illness.

Each generation in all societies, large or small, civilized or primitive, learns feelings that seem most effective both for surviving and for staying involved. As children we learn that when someone frustrates or angers us we cannot impulsively lash out as the angry feelings may urge us. If we do, our parents teach us that we will have little chance for security or success, as in earlier times they taught us to restrain ourselves to survive. The thoughtless, impulsive response is unsuited to the cooperation necessary to survive or to succeed in any society, primitive or modern. Therefore, to live successfully with others, we learn early to modify our behavior, to respond carefully to the immediate urges of common feelings such as anger. When we cannot express anger directly at the person or situation that angers us, we may hurt someone who did not anger us ("kicking the cat"), develop a psychosomatic symptom (back pain is very common), or anesthetize the anger through alcohol or drugs.

Perhaps the most common alternative to anger is depression, which contains and controls the anger. We have learned from previous, apparently similar situations to become depressed, to hold the anger within us because we would probably be rejected, hurt, or frustrated if we lashed out. Characteristically, depression feels different from anger and stimulates a different response. We tend to become more withdrawn, more inert, and more capable of harming ourselves than someone else. We can thus usually avoid both a direct reprisal (few people will hurt us when we are depressed) and alienating those we believe we need. And, at least for a while, others usually pay attention to our suffering. If we solve the frustration that caused the anger without antagonizing those we need, the depression soon passes; the brief depression, painful as it was, helped us. If, however, we do not learn how to relieve the underlying anger or frustration without losing those we need, we will remain depressed.

Besides depression, we learn other emotions that reduce, dilute, or can be substituted for the pain of anger or fear. Tension, anxiety, fatigue, boredom, and psychosomatic symptoms are feelings we have learned to experience when we are angry or frightened. Some of us learn to respond to these feelings by behaving in ways that increase our involvement or security, which in turn reduces the pain. Many of us do not; the pain continues because, in response to our feelings, we have learned behavior that decreases rather than increases our involvement or security. To illustrate, at times it may be advantageous to be strongly assertive when angered, as, for example, when our boss passes us over for a raise. Rather than passively acquiesce and become depressed, which may cause him to respect us less, we should stand up and tell him what we have done that deserves more money. If our family rejected us as children every time we became assertive, however, we may have learned only to become depressed. Such training serves us poorly later. It follows, therefore, that the more successful our family and friends, the better chance we have to learn behavior that leads to success. Because of this behavior, as we grow we experience feelings that further urge us to behave responsibility. It is a circle: the more responsibly we behave, the better we feel; the better we feel, the more responsibly we behave.

People with successful identities usually behave under stress in ways that cause pain to decrease and later enable them to experience pleasure. Successful people characteristically learn to suppress the immediate, angry emotion. Although they know when to be assertive and aggressive, they do so without the anger that may reduce or destroy needed involvement. They can stand up for their rights without getting into an irrational argument because they have learned that as long as they stay involved, the painful feelings will dissipate. When attacked or rejected, they usually respond with consideration, thus blunting the attack and making themselves harder to reject. Successful people learn to cope with anger or its civilized derivatives, such as depression and anxiety, quickly and effectively by working to turn the situation toward involvement. Knowing from experience that good feelings are possible, they learn behavior that creates pleasure rather than pain. In the public schools I often meet teachers who, frustrated by antagonistic or nonlearning children, respond to them with anger or depression. The teachers are pleased when we show them how to get involved as friends with the same children who previously irritated them. Through the good feelings that everyone then has, they can motivate the children toward learning. It is the teacher's responsibility, however, to make the first move toward involvement.

Failures, on the other hand, usually respond impulsively to anger, often decreasing both their security and their involvement. As a result they experience more and more pain and they search in increasing desperation for relief. When social pressures or rules limit their anger, they, like successes, learn to modify their feelings to reduce frustration. But, because they do not know how to handle anger or frustration effectively by working toward involvement, they find it difficult to get rid of painful feelings. Anger, for example, more often becomes depression for people who are failures than it does for people who are successes. Unable to become involved with others, they may remain depressed for long periods. As they continue to be depressed, it becomes harder for them to work toward involvement. In addition their depression acts as a discouraging barrier for anyone who tries to get involved with them.

Failures, suffering in many ways for long periods, seldom learn from their pain to behave more responsibly. Millions of unhappily married couples, for example, respond to each other with irritation and anger because they do not know how to do otherwise. Starving for love, they give each other only pain. Frustrated in their locked-in relationship and pushed by painful feelings, they either act quickly and thoughtlessly or do nothing except wallow in their own suffering. The pain, which should serve as a warning to change their behavior toward each other, only pushes them further apart. As failures, they succumb year after year, in one situation after another, to the immediate urge to fight or withdraw, which does temporarily lessen the pain but does nothing to solve the loneliness that caused the pain. To make their marriage better, each must learn to respond to hostility with kindness and love, a response they have not learned—and unfortunately most believe that they cannot learn it in this marriage.

In the new identity society, the most common cause of pain is the failure to get involved, which we experience as loneliness. Although we suffer a great deal when we are angry or fearful, we ordinarily resolve these feelings without losing involvement. If we do not, we may eventually become uninvolved or lonely. But we can also fail to become involved without ever feeling anger or fear. Trying to reduce the pain of loneliness, we may suffer depression, jealousy, suspicion, greed, revenge, hate, guilt, shame, and boredom. *Although all these feelings are painful, none is as painful as becoming directly aware that we are alone, rejecting and rejected by others around us.* If we are unable to substitute any of these common feelings for the pain of loneliness and if we remain uninvolved, our nervous system may become so overwhelmed with the pain of loneliness that we choose to escape into unreality. We deny reality itself to reduce the pain. A long solitary confinement may cause people to become "stir-crazy," prison jargon for getting rid of the pain of loneliness by leaving reality. In a sense, almost all inmates of mental hospitals are "stir-crazy"; they are attempting to flee a lonely prison of their own making. Other people may react to the pain of loneliness by behaving in hostile, aggressive, unfeeling ways. The con man, for example, gains the confidence of others to bilk them. In his loneliness, he sees no value to other people except to use or to exploit them. Most antisocial behavior is an attempt to reduce the pain of loneliness by hurting or exploiting others. Those hurt often have nothing to do with the loneliness of the criminal or con man; he hates them just because they are people with whom he cannot become involved.

In the everyday lives of many lonely people the pain is constant and gnawing. Discouraged because they do not believe they can get involved, many respond to the urge to escape the pain by taking what seems to them the best choice available for relief from the nagging ache. More than twenty million people in this country use alcohol or drugs regularly, both of which do relieve the pain—until the effect wears off.

Pleasure may also be examined further. In the primitive survival society, most feelings of pleasure, except for sex, were experienced as relief from pain; when we hurt, we did what we could to reduce the pain. If we were successful, not only did the pain cease, but as it went away we began to feel good. If we have been sick with the flu, as soon as we start to feel well—the aching in our muscles lessens, our back loosens up, our cough diminishes, and our fever drops—we feel good although we may still be weak. As the pain diminishes, nature encourages us with pleasure to continue what we are doing that is helping our recovery. Something as simple as a glass of cool water can provide great pleasure when we are hot and thirsty. Countless similar examples of pleasurable feeling still occur today that must have been present from the beginnings of our existence.

This form of pleasure, perhaps better called relief, is experienced only in relationship to pain. It is not available unless it is preceded by pain, and it is limited to the extent that it is contrasted to pain. When we are a little thirsty, for example, a cool glass of water is a mild pleasure; as our thirst increases, so does the pleasure of relief. The pleasure associated with relief is rarely directly motivating: we would not ordinarily refuse water to gain the relief of quenching our thirst. Enjoyable as relief is, we are mainly motivated by the pain; pleasure or relief is an extra.

One great pleasure, sex, is not associated with relief of pain. Sexual activity is almost purely pleasurable. The pain associated with the lack of sex cannot be compared with the immediate and direct pain associated with hunger, cold, thirst, or injury. The pain we associate with the absence of sex is really the pain of loneliness. Sex with someone we care for is always enjoyable.

Although sex may have been the first purely pleasurable feeling, as we gained security and had time to enjoy each other's company, to engage in primitive games, and to laugh with each other, we soon discovered the social pleasures and good feelings inherent to involvement itself. We now sought company not because we were driven toward each other by the pangs and dangers of loneliness but because we discovered many ways besides sex and not related to the relief of pain to become involved with and enjoy each other. It did not really hurt to stand back from the games, dances, and rituals, but it was fun to participate. Although we could enjoy watching others, we soon found that when we danced, when we played the games, when we worked toward the emerging, complicated, personal relationships, we felt better.

One pleasure, laughter, merits a brief discussion. Successful, involved people, primitive or civilized, laugh a great deal; their self-confidence in their successful identity enables them to laugh at themselves. Many of us can laugh at others and at situations outside ourselves; not so many of us can laugh at ourselves, at our own foibles or pomp. To see humor in man's struggle is not, as dour people accuse, a lack of seriousness or concern. The more we are able to laugh, the less oppressive and overwhelming becomes the struggle. It is good to be able to see oneself as a human being and to see clearly the difficult struggle to help others in a reality sometimes intolerable without laughter. A person who cannot laugh at all, or who laughs only at others, is often a failure. A person who can laugh at himself and at the world he is struggling to improve is usually highly involved, confident, and successful.

The pain and the resultant relief when the pain was gone occurred swiftly in the primitive society. In the primitive identity society we learned to delay the urge for immediate pleasure so that, through planning and patience, we might experience greater pleasure later. We derived more pleasure by working hard to create a better tool, weapon, or work of art than we did by making a slipshod, short-term effort. Although planning and carrying out a project was often not enjoyable and was often painfully lonely, we gained more worthwhile recognition and involvement in the end than a quick, haphazard effort would have afforded. The Little Red Hen gained pleasure by saving grain that she could have eaten immediately and then baking it into delicious bread.

The pleasure of long-term involvement and the achievement of difficult goals motivate successful people. In contrast, those who fail are lonely and settle for easily achievable goals of drinking or fighting. They experience little pleasure; they are primarily motivated by the prospect of temporary relief of pain and the transitory pleasure that accompanies it. Failures who use drugs or alcohol to replace the human involvements they need to gain a successful identity only lock themselves further into failure. For successful people, however, the moderate social use of alcohol or another mild drug will often provide a pleasure not tied to the relief of pain, a pleasure that develops as the drug or alcohol helps increase the social facility we are confident we have. Similarly, the few remaining primitive people unaffected by contact with civilized societies use drugs or alcohol for the pleasure they add to periodic ceremonies. On the other hand, men of primitive societies whose culture has been destroyed by civilization may use drugs and alcohol excessively to escape the pain they feel when they discover the loss of their own society and cannot adjust to civilization.

Early man learned well the pleasurable involvement possible through complex kinship systems, religion and ritual, art and music, dances and games. These means of involvement reached their peak in many uncrowded, abundant, primitive societies in which there was time for many pleasurable group activities and no emphasis on private property or personal power. Our new identity society is faced with the dilemma of quickly providing involvement-oriented schools and jobs by using the institutions and social systems of the previous survival society that subordinated involvement to the struggle to survive. If we had not already made a good beginning, particularly in plentiful good-paying jobs, we would not even be entering the new society. The challenge now is to develop in a few years a social system that will provide us pathways toward success through the pleasure of involvement. We must change the habits of 10,000 years of civilization in which the goal was security and the main motivation was pain.

Certainly there were lonely people in the primitive cultures, but culture itself was based upon involvement and its attendant pleasures. Initiation and adolescence rites helped young people gain a successful identity and a place as a valuable member of the society. Today we have few ceremonies geared to increased involvement that initiate people into the civilized identity society. The new identity society does not accept a person just because he comes of age. Although a high school or college diploma does provide evidence of adulthood, the evidence is more negative than positive; that is, although not having a diploma often leads to rejection and consequent failure, having one is no guarantee of acceptance or success.

Despite fewer pathways to involvement today than in the primitive identity society, many people do succeed and are motivated mainly by pleasure. They may encounter rejection and loneliness that hurt, but the pain is not so overwhelming that they react impulsively. They can bear the pain because they know they are working to make friends and to do something worthwhile. Their motivation rests in their confidence that the pain will subside and be replaced by the pleasure of involvement. In contrast, a person who identifies himself as a failure, who has no confidence in his ability to get involved, always feels a great deal of pain. He is motivated by the pain to do something quickly that, though it may reduce the pain, does not get him involved.

For example, a man with family, friends, and success at work can often suffer a death in his family or the loss of a good job and still, with the confidence that says, "I am successful and I still have friends," rebuild his life. He is motivated by his self-confidence that he is capable of involvement and worthwhile work and his knowledge from previous pleasures that pleasure is available to him through these pathways. Although he does not deny or ignore the pain, he does not try to rid himself of it quickly and irrationally; instead he plans thoughtfully to gain new relationships. He has learned not to be misled by pain. It is present, acute, and upsetting, but he understands the cause and is confident he knows how to resolve it. Unwilling to settle for a lesser temporary pleasure by just relieving the pain, he works toward a greater pleasure by responsibly reordering his life to maintain his successful identity.

Another man suffering the same misfortune and the same pain may, in his misery, begin to avoid his friends. As he does, he will lose confidence in himself and believe he will never be able to replace the person or opportunity he has lost. Forgetting the pleasure of his previous life, he becomes motivated to reduce the pain quickly. He may even choose to deny entirely the need to find new relationships or a new job. Sitting at home, doing nothing, and saying there is nothing he can do will provide him temporary surcease from his belief that he no longer has a chance for success. Arthur Miller's play *The Price* takes place in the house of a man who did this after the crash of 1929. In both examples, above, when the going was easy the men appeared to be successful. The difference is that the first man was deeply involved and had a successful identity that could withstand stress. The second man had limited involvement and, under stress, identified with failure. Consequently he behaved as a failure to reduce the pain.

It is often remarked (erroneously, I believe) that in today's identity society people have less strength and stamina than they used to have; this loss is attributed to overconcern with personal pleasure. Years ago most people settled for dull, monotonous lives because they did not believe a better life was possible. A man did not toil in an ill-paying job because of strength of character; he did so because he believed that to survive he had no other option. Rarely enjoying the toil, he often drank a great deal when he could. The British Navy only recently cut out its grog ration. The grog made bearable the inhuman conditions in the old Royal Navy.

The pain of insecurity and the relief gained by security drove most people to work hard in the survival society. The expectation of little pleasure was judged as fortitude, which it probably was. Workers received some "honest yeoman" reinforcement from the power structure for taking life's knocks with an uncomplaining smile. There is no special virtue, however, to bearing what must be borne. It probably takes equal fortitude to become involved and develop a strong independent role, as Albert Schweitzer demonstrated in Lambaréné. In the survival society pleasure, so important to us, was considered frivolous, unnecessary, and immoral. This Puritan attitude was a serviceable rationale for lives filled with loneliness and misery. The rationale helped people who accepted it reduce the pain caused by suppressing the need for involvement.

Now we are in an identity society that places great emphasis on personal pleasure. Finding little virtue in hard work for security and survival alone, people do work hard if work reinforces their humanity. Given the security, or the illusion of it, of the identity society, we seek the pleasure of a successful identity. If we are unable to gain a successful identity, our only retreat is to failure. The half-billion people who have achieved security since about 1950 must now either gain a successful identity or suffer the pain of a failure identity. True, some people are still insecure, especially if they are out of work, but few of them are concerned about starving; their main concern is the drop in the quality of their lives, not life itself. Certainly this attitude is borne out by our current energy shortage. High prices for fuel will somewhat lower our standard of living, but they will hardly put us back into the survival culture.

The huge number of people who today identify themselves as failures and who, because of the pain of their loneliness, suffer or cause others to suffer, represent a condition totally new to mankind. Never before have so many people struggled for personal fulfillment unsuccessfully. Although there were identity failures in previous societies, they were few in number because only a few people at the top were even concerned about identity; most people settled for security and hoped for limited fulfillment. The large numbers on the bottom had little or no fulfillment because all their efforts were in trying to survive.

Now, because we are entering the identity society so rapidly and because we do not have enough social pathways to success, we actually have two societies: the failure society, those who identify themselves as failures and are motivated by pain to reduce the pain in ways that do not lead to involvement; and the success society, those who identify themselves as successes and are motivated by pleasure to become more involved.

When we are involved as friends or as lovers, we feel pleasure. Movement toward others produces the initial pleasure that motivates us to increase the involvement. When we are involved, our pleasureful feelings rise or fall as we move toward or away from those we care for. If we believe ourselves to be secure, we always gain pleasures as we move toward someone new. We always suffer pain as we move away from someone with whom we are involved. When a child runs happily down the street to meet his father coming home from work and the father holds out his arms toward the child, there is always joy. When a wife kisses her husband good-by and waves him off to war, there is always sadness. When lovers part and move away, there can be no happiness. Those who identify themselves as successes in our society are able to move toward other people and keep the movement going. Those who identify themselves as failures move away from others and think that they cannot move toward another person.

Conflict arises when we must make a decision to move closer to one person at the expense of moving away from another. Typical examples are an executive who must decide between two qualified persons for a promotion, a coach between two good quarterbacks, or a mother and daughter between whom to include and whom to drop from a wedding guest list. There is no difference between the choice that is forced, as in the above examples, or the choice that is voluntary, as in the case of a wife who chooses between her husband and another man. These choices are especially unpleasant if the intensity of the involvement is or has been high. We feel pain when we lose or move rapidly away from anyone, even temporarily. Delaying or refusing to make a necessary decision to move away, sometimes with the hope that the decision will not be necessary, only increases our pain. An example is a girl who must decide whether or not to continue an affair without commitment when she wants a commitment. The only way for her to get a commitment from the man is to separate or threaten credibly to separate. If she does not get the commitment, she has still gained because she will not be wasting time with that man in the future.

People with successful identities make the choice and enjoy

the pleasure of whatever closeness the choice produces. They can withstand the pain of the separation because they know, once the choice is made, the pain will subside. Failures, on the other hand, refuse to choose and agonize over the decision. They suffer increased pain as they become involved with the decision itself and lose involvement with the people the decision concerns. When a choice must be made, we should not reject the loser excessively or spitefully and thus add to both his and our pain. Recognizing the desirability of reducing the pain of separation, California recently passed a divorce law in which fault has been eliminated. The state wisely decided that, painful as dissolving marriage is, it is far worse to assign blame and thus increase the rejection and, consequently, the pain and the failure.

The degree of pleasure attained when people come together depends upon three facets of the relationship: speed, quality, and depth. To explain speed, consider two people who have no reason to fear each other moving rapidly together. Their pleasure is increased and their involvement is heightened by the speed of the process; the faster they move together, the better they feel. Although rapid movement together cannot continue indefinitely, the pleasure is highest during the time of greatest speed. Quality occurs and pleasure increases in a relationship if two people value each other highly and believe each other to be worthwhile and loving. A man moving toward a woman who is capable, intelligent, and particular of her associates will experience greater pleasure than if he moves toward a less attractive woman.

The example may be continued to explain depth. Depth is present if the young man and woman moving toward each other are able to communicate easily, to plan together, to have some common goals, to reinforce each other's values, and to become not only physically involved with each other but also intellectually involved together with ideas and projects, sports and games, and hobbies and possessions. The greater the depth of their relationship, the greater the pleasure. If two people moving toward each other find they have few mutual interests, the relationship has little depth. The briefly intense pleasure, including that of the sexual relationship, is rapidly dissipated. Speed, which has little to do with personal qualities, can nevertheless by itself produce a short intense relationship, as many disillusioned weekend lovers will testify. Although quality and speed may both exist in many celebrated, short-lived marriages such as commonly occur in show business, the couple may have little in common besides fame (not an easy quality to share). Therefore, no depth develops and the marriage rapidly falls apart. Both were and are valuable people, but they were unable or unwilling to work toward developing depth in the relationship. Speed and quality will build and increase pleasure in a relationship for a while, but depth makes the relationship last.

In summary, when we feel bad, we must learn not to try to reduce the pain in a way that separates us from others. We must learn to work toward involvement, even when it takes time. Although we may suffer lonely, painful periods as we discover ways to increase our involvement, confidence that we will eventually be involved will make these periods less lonely and painful. As we grow and mature, we can increase our pleasure by making the necessary effort to keep and to deepen the good involvements that we have. Many lonely people, in despair of ever achieving good long-term involvements, become involved solely with themselves. They cannot distinguish between the long-term pleasures of a successful identity and the brief erratic pleasures useful only to relieve pain.

Chapter Three

Loneliness and Failure

Our new society, fraught with loneliness and failure, is more concerned with relief of pain and suffering than any previous time. One-quarter of all medical prescriptions are for tranquilizers or pain-relieving drugs. More than half of the people who see physicians do so for nonspecific complaints rather than for definite physical ailments. Our newspapers are full of advertisements urging lonely people, who may be despondent with the pain of loneliness, to call the Help Line or the Hot Line. If you cannot find love, you can call a dating service and a computer will match you to another lonely person. If your loneliness and irresponsibility fall into one of several common patterns, you may join an old, established group such as Alcoholics Anonymous or a new group such as Recovery Incorporated, Gamblers Anonymous, Synanon, or Neurotics Anonymous. All these groups bring lonely people together to relieve their suffering caused by loneliness and failure by getting them to help one another become more responsible through mutual involvement.

In the identity society many group movements try to involve those who feel lonely and help those already involved become more effective in their relationships. Unlike Alcoholics Anonymous, these groups do not deal with specific forms of failure. Under the general names of sensitivity training or encounter groups, they are represented by institutions such as the National Training Lab in Bethel, Maine, and the newer, more "popular" institution, Esalen in Big Sur, California. Numerous similar institutions sponsor a wide variety of groups, such as executives groups, singles groups, and married groups, that help people gain involvement for brief or extended periods. Many churches have embarked on widespread counseling and guidance efforts, and many ministers spend as much time counseling and guiding their flock as they do spreading the gospel. The established professions of psychiatry, psychology, and social work are now augmented by semiprofessional agencies such as halfway houses, retreat houses, and settlement houses that attempt to help or replace certificated social science professionals. Serving a wide variety of people who do not want or cannot afford professional help, these agencies provide a setting somewhat similar to that of a family where people can escape their loneliness and perhaps find reasonable involvement with other lonely people.

Alcohol continues in wide use. In addition, with affluence and increased access to physicians, millions of people are using other drugs of all kinds, legal and illegal, in an attempt to relieve the pain of failure. Despite all the people helping to relieve pain, many of whom understand that the pain, whatever its form, is a result of loneliness and failure to gain a successful identity, we are making little headway in reaching the many people who need help. Even under the best conditions, with a good therapist who knows how to get involved and a motivated client who understands the need to change his behavior toward more involvement, changing from failure to success is very hard. Under the worst conditions of chronic failure—an alcoholic, a drug addict, or a long-term psychotic —changing from failure to success is almost impossible. The question must be raised: Why is it so hard? Why is a failure identity, accompanied by so much pain, so hard to change? What purpose does hostile behavior or withdrawal serve? They must have a very important purpose, or people would not cling to them so tenaciously. Why are drugs and alcohol so valuable that people will not give them up even when they understand how destructive they are?

The need for involvement has been built into our nervous systems and we always feel pain when we have none. The pain warns us to seek involvement with others. If we fail in the attempt, there is always one possibility left for involvement: ourselves. Unsatisfactory and painful as this is in comparison with involvement with others who are worthwhile, involvement with ourselves will reduce and sometimes even eliminate temporarily the pain of being alone. But because we need involvement with others, self-involvement is an inadequate alternative; we cannot fool our nervous system for long. Quickly dissatisfied with our self-involvement, it again responds with pain and we respond with further self-deception in response to the pain.

To avoid the fact that we are really involved with ourselves, we have learned to focus our attention on a creation outside ourselves. We create and then concentrate on an idea, such as an obsessive fear of germs; a behavior, such as compulsive gambling; a physical symptom, such as migraine headache; or an emotion such as depression. We focus on these self-creations as if they were real and separate from us. Keeping overly clean, gambling, suffering and treating a headache, or being depressed then becomes our problem in place of our true problem—that we need others. We have *chosen* to act as we do because we desperately hope the symptom or the behavior will provide enough involvement to satisfy what we should get from others. We create the symptom or behavior and then, to keep it outside of ourselves, attempt to deny to ourselves that the behavior is our own choice. Our nervous system accepts our self-created symptoms or behavior as companions because they do reduce the pain, sometimes for long periods and because we give ourselves no other choice. Occasionally the symptom or behavior can provide enough involvement not only to relieve the pain of loneliness but actually to give brief pleasure. Therefore, no matter what we choose, when we are able to develop involvements with our own symptoms instead of with other people the pain of loneliness is reduced, as if the symptom or behavior were itself someone else. Over thousands of years of loneliness, we have developed numberless self-involved symptoms and behaviors to keep us company and reduce the pain of loneliness. Whether we choose a painful involvement, such as depression, or a somewhat enjoyable one, as alcoholism sometimes is in its early stages, we at least have some involvement with something of our own creation that will not desert us.

For failing people who do not believe the pleasure of responsible involvement is open, becoming involved with themselves and then with creations of themselves is less painful than facing the reality of their loneliness. Despite the inability of self-involvement to produce lasting good feelings, its ready availability leads those who fail to conclude wrongly that they have made the best of a bad situation. This conclusion would be correct only if it were impossible for them to get involved with other people, but this is almost never the case. However, failures with no recent experience of involvement with others have little confidence that they can become involved. Eventually they choose what appears to them to be their only option: themselves.

Extreme intellectual attention to our own ideas and feelings is one kind of self-involvement. In the play *Othello,* Iago, involved with his hatred of Othello, creates cunning schemes to destroy the Moor. Hamlet, enmeshed in rejection and loneliness, listens only to those who reinforce these feelings. In each case, as their self-involvement increases, the motivating pain of loneliness is temporarily reduced; nevertheless, as the plays unfold, both Hamlet and Iago increasingly shut others out. Their final irrational behavior precludes any recognition of the existence of others. They consider only their own ideas, behavior, and feelings.

The world is full of would-be Hamlets and Iagos who, though seldom as successful as the literary characters at gaining the intense self-involvement and full companionship that their own rationalizations and feelings provide, do succeed enough to make them very hard to reach. Both Iago and Hamlet were able to become deeply involved with a product of themselves, Iago with his scheming and evil cunning, Hamlet with his melancholy and irrational revenge. Neither gained pleasure from his actions, but both were intensely motivated by the belief that they were compelled to act as they did. They justified their actions on the basis of their own feelings of being wronged, rejected, and isolated.

Though both Iago and Hamlet were initially lonely, their subsequent behavior increased their isolation. Everything they did reinforced their decision to become involved with themselves, with their own intellect, emotions, scheming, and revenge, to the exclusion of all other people. They are classic examples of failures who replace their loneliness with a self-created idea, behavior, symptom, or emotion.

Everyone knows people with this kind of self-involvement who talk about their symptoms, problems, feelings, or behavior as if they were alive in their own right. Many difficulties are permanent companions; others come and go. A person may say, "My headache is back," as if it went on vacation and then suddenly returned. Seemingly, the person had no responsibility for its reappearance; it just decided to come back on its own. Backache, stomachache, depression, compulsion, hallucination, delusion, and extreme fear of someone or something are all examples of the thousands of self-created companions that keep us company in a variety of ways. Some of these companions are so interesting that we have assigned them Greek names; we call them phobias as in claustrophobia (the fear of being enclosed), or manias, as in kleptomania (the uncontrollable urge to steal). I believe *every* psychologically diagnosable condition is an example of involvement with one's own idea, behavior, symptom, or emotion, or some combination of them.

People frequently rationalize their involvement with their self-created companions. For example, in kleptomania (involvement with stealing) the desire to steal becomes irresistible because the act of thievery reduces the pain. When caught, the person is willing to accept the psychiatric rationalization that his self-involvement is a disease that has attacked him from the outside, like typhoid fever, because it is less painful to be treated kindly as a poor unfortunate kleptomaniac than to be locked up as a thief.

All of these self-involvements are companions that we choose to become involved with in our attempt to ease the pain that results from failure. Some of them are more successful than others in relieving pain. If these symptoms or behaviors do not serve to extinguish the pain, and many do not (certainly Hamlet suffered), they at least allow us to localize it. Rather than becoming involved with an overwhelming and pervasive sense of loneliness, we can become involved with a focused pain or behavior that we can discuss and perhaps rationalize and understand. We can live more comfortably with a painful but discreet and faithful companion than with loneliness.

Consider as an example a most common symptom, depression. Everyone has been depressed for some time in his life. Depression frequently occurs when we are rejected. Sometimes, as I have explained in Chapter Two, it replaces socially unacceptable anger. We often become depressed when we lose a needed or desirable job or when someone we love dies. Losing a job can illustrate the mechanism of the companionship of depression. Because we are deprived of our livelihood, our self-esteem is lowered. We believe that we have lost value in the eyes of those who are dependent on us, or if we have no dependents who are important to us, we lose value in our own eyes. No matter how little we think the job loss was our fault, we keep going over what we might have done to keep it and thus blame ourselves as well as others.

If we cannot soon find an equally good job, we tend to avoid others who work successfully. We may shun members of our family because we want neither their sympathy nor their scorn. As we lose value in our own eyes, as we separate from others, and as we suffer painful feelings of loneliness and incompetence, we become depressed. Painful as the depression is, it is less painful than facing the reality of our situation. The depression also provides us with a secondary benefit. It allows us to be withdrawn and somewhat immobilized and therefore temporarily excused from the hard work of starting over. The more we are at fault, the more depressed we are. Attempting to use the depression as a substitute for the involvement, the companionship, and the value we acquired through the job, we will remain depressed until we can get another one. Unfortunately, the depression makes it less likely that we will get another job, although it does make the period of unemployment somewhat more bearable.

A little depression from time to time is normal; most people recover and again move toward others. Staying depressed for a long time, however, signifies our inability to gain new involvements to replace the old ones. The depression now becomes a friend, not a good friend, but a faithful foul-weather friend whom we can always count on, a friend, who if we are incompetent, may consume all of our time to the point of immobilizing us with his friendship.

People with successful identities, with many friends and responsible involvements, certainly become depressed when they lose someone through death, when they are separated from someone they value, when they lose an opportunity, or even when they are involved in accidents. They do not welcome the depression, however; they use it as a warning to think their loss through clearly and reasonably. They may decide, "Well, this is something that's happened to me. Certainly I'm depressed, but I'd better get going and do something constructive." They have the ability to make new involvements, to plan to overcome whatever happened to them so that they do not remain depressed and lose involvement with people for whom they care. They also look for new involvements. Keeping old involvements and making new ones take effort, planning, confidence, and experience.

Most people learn to work for reinvolvement; they are motivated by pleasure, and they believe they can overcome losses and rejections. Failing people or people with only one close attachment that is lost cannot overcome a major loss. They may spend much time sighing, moaning, and complaining. They may say half-heartedly, "I would go out and look for friends, but I'm so tired, so upset, and so depressed that I won't or I can't or who would want me like this?" Involved with their complaining and their misery, they use them as an excuse for not doing what they should do. They often remain depressed for long periods.

Remaining depressed, although an excellent rationalization for inaction, is still painful. Everyone wants to end the pain and the suffering. One way, the best way, is to get involved, but failing people have no confidence in their ability to find other people, and in their depressed state, they may not even understand that they must do so. Today, however, the constant barrage of ads for pain-relieving medications tells us all that we need not suffer. Although the drugs will relieve the pain, they then become in themselves a new companion, replacing the painful old companion of depression.

Probably some pills are necessary for failures who are doing little to get involved. If they were to face the reality of their inadequacy—they are not moving toward friends or they have few friends; that most people avoid them in their depressed state; a few people treat them kindly but as an incompetent child—the pain would be unbearable. To face this pain either without the companion of depression or with the companion but without the pills to relieve its pain would be so overwhelming that they might attempt suicide. Although depression insulates failures from reality, it, like all other symptoms of failure behavior that do the same thing, may cause great pain itself. If the failing person cannot find a more satisfactory symptom, he may try something quick and simple to get rid of the pain. Both old and new means are available to relieve the pain quickly and simply, if temporarily. Old ways are alcohol and plant-derived drugs; newer ways are chemically produced drugs.

Most medical practice is based on relieving pain. Today millions of people go to doctors in an attempt to relieve the pain of depression and its close relatives—a host of nagging, painful complaints such as fatigue, headache, intestinal upset, muscular aches, and loss of interest in sex. Many doctors, however, do not understand that depression and most other such symptoms and complaints are companions. Trained to get rid of pain, they respond to the complaints of failing people by prescribing drugs and medications that treat the aching companion but not the social incompetence and the lack of involvement that cause the symptom. Pharmaceutical companies are engaged in frenetic research to find tranquilizers, drugs, and painkillers to fill the demand. They face an impossible job. Each new pill and tranquilizer becomes a fresh, highly touted friend that, like the last "friend," soon deserts the failing person. Though different, the new becomes the old and the pain returns. A pill can never replace a friend. Very few doctors have both the time and the desire to get involved with their patients and guide them toward new, close, responsible involvements and worthwhile behavior. Doctors are trained to respond to pain and symptoms with medication and surgery, and that is what they do. Fortunately, extreme procedures such as lobotomies and electric shock treatments are used less now than formerly because it has become clear that they often do more harm than good.

Many people who do not see doctors or who see them and get little relief use alcohol, our old, reliable, all-purpose pain reliever, and drugs, legal and illegal. No matter how many pain relievers we outlaw or suppress, others will take their place because failing people are in a desperate search for something new to alleviate their painful symptoms, the companions they desperately choose to avoid facing loneliness and failure.

Drugs are harmful for people with failure identities because they make the loneliness, the failure, and the self-involvement tolerable. In doing so, the drugs negate the purpose of the pain: to warn us that our companion, self-involvement, is working poorly at best. They allow us to sit on the hot stove and not feel the pain even though we know we are being burned. When the effect wears off, failing people quickly take more drugs or alcohol, which, in relieving the pain temporarily, becomes the new companion. Very quickly a new involvement begins that replaces the symptom or the behavior that was the previous and less effective companion. Asking an alcoholic to give up his alcohol is as effective as asking a man on a hot stove to sit still until the stove cools off. Preaching about, educating against, and banning drugs and alcohol will not effectively limit their use by those with failure identities. We will eliminate them only by eliminating failure, the inadequacy to find the involvement necessary in this society. When the pain of failure is anesthetized, the best motivation to become responsibly involved is removed. The more ingenious our society is at finding pain relievers, the less progress we will make toward helping failing people find the success that will produce pleasure.

The drug used to alleviate the pain of a failure identity thus becomes itself an obstacle to gaining the human involvement necessary for a successful identity. A mental patient locked in a state hospital with no program for guidance toward responsible involvements will not be helped to give up his symptoms by drugs. The drug may calm his crazy symptoms and make them less painful, it may make the ward he lives on quieter, and it may make the work of the staff easier. None of these reasons by itself justifies the use of the drug. However, when this quieter and calmer atmosphere helps the hospital develop a program for patient involvement and worthwhile work, moderate use of drugs does serve a purpose. When the hospital has such a program, as all hospitals should, the use of tranquilizers to help patients calm down and become involved in the program is wise. In a hospital with such a program, the administration of tranquilizing drugs to patients often encourages the staff, who identify quiet and passivity with less craziness, to try harder to reach the patients.

For a person with a success identity suffering from temporary loneliness or stress, the relief of pain can provide a needed respite that helps him endure the rejections, disappointments, and hazards of our inconsistent reality. As long as he knows that he is consciously gaining relief and not denying the reality of his life, there is no reason to deny him a few drinks, an aspirin, or an occasional sleeping pill or tranquilizer.

For people who identify themselves as failures, however, what seems to be reasonable is often dangerous. Many apparently responsible individuals commit suicide with a prescribed barbiturate. It is not too much to ask that doctors, before prescribing large quantities of pain-relieving drugs, interview the patient to discover whether he identifies himself as successful or failing. Finding out is not difficult. A few questions about the patient's social life and his work can easily reveal whether he is lonely, feels worthless, has few positive involvements, and has developed one or more symptomatic or behavioral self-involvements to replace people with whom he should be involved. One question the doctor should ask is:

"When did you recently have a really good time?" If the patient cannot answer that question positively, the doctor should be cautious about prescribing tranquilizers or narcotics. Instead, he should urge the patient to get some kind of help toward becoming more involved.

There is much mid-ground between the position of a failure who depends on drugs or alcohol for his only friend and the position of a highly involved person who drinks an occasional cocktail or takes an occasional sleeping pill or aspirin. The heavy drinker who is not alcoholic, who has many friends, and who functions well in the world likes the feeling of relief from the realistic tensions of a striving life that alcohol gives. He is able to control his drinking, heavy though it is. Thus heavy drinking is not always an indication of limited involvement, loneliness, and failure. Similarly, heavy smokers or big eaters who are overweight are not necessarily using cigarettes or food to replace human involvement. Among such people are successful people; they are not relieving the pain of failure and they are not losing touch with reality. Many who use drugs or alcohol heavily continue as they are for years because they have learned to use them for whatever pleasure they provide. Though the alcohol or drugs may be companions, they are not replacements for human companions.

A positive use of drugs—converting heroin addicts to methadone—now has many supporters. Many intelligent people believe that most heroin addicts will never be able to gain or maintain the kind of responsible involvements that will make life without any drugs possible. There are some addicts who, living in a sheltered and well-supervised environment like Synanon, can become involved enough to live without drugs, but they need to remain in the environment. Those who advocate methadone as a legal substitute for heroin believe correcily that many addicts would refuse to move into a place like Synanon for life, even if there were enough room for them. They think the practical thing to do is give the addicts relief with a less debilitating drug in their own homes or in clinics, and methadone is the drug of choice.

Basic to the task of convincing the authorities that methadone is an acceptable substitute for heroin is to assure them that it does not produce pleasure. Because even heroin does not produce any significant pleasure other than the relief of pain, this should be easy. The trouble is that many people think that heroin is a strong pleasure-producing drug, and they suspect that any drug that can replace it must be the same. Methadone does not produce pleasure any more than heroin does. It probably does not even relieve pain as effectively as heroin; however, it does relieve enough pain to convince many heroin addicts to give up the struggle to get heroin. They decide that the slight extra pain reduction heroin provides is not worth the cost and effort of obtaining it. They settle for methadone, which reduces the pain to a tolerable level and is provided free. Obviously, a program that teaches responsible involvement and enables addicts to give up even the use of methadone would be best, but we have not yet found a successful program to do this. If the methadone helps them tolerate their loneliness, get a job, and stop preying on society or their relatives for the fifty to one hundred dollars a day that they need for heroin, the benefit is great.

Obsessions, compulsions, psychoses, and most long-term symptomatic illnesses that have no presently known medical cause all serve the same purpose as depression. They act as companions that lonely people *choose* because they are unable to tolerate the knowledge that they have only themselves with whom to become involved, knowledge that might lead to suicide if a symptom companion cannot be developed or relief cannot be obtained for the pain. Many reasonable people take exception to the word "choose." They say a man can choose to behave in hostile and antagonistic ways, but he cannot choose to have a stomach ulcer, he cannot choose to go crazy, he cannot choose to be frightened of airplanes, and he cannot choose to be depressed.

Nevertheless, I believe that in most cases these behaviors or symptoms are indeed chosen. For ninety years "modern" psychiatry has conditioned us to the idea that if we suffer from psychological symptoms there is little choice involved; the symptom and the pain are the result of a conflict rooted in our subconscious mind, a part of our mind over which we have no control. Certainly we have a lifetime of experiences, many long forgotten and residing in our subconscious mind, that help determine what symptoms we choose, but in almost every case *we have the symptom now because we are lonely and failing now.* Certainly, a careful history of a failing person can reveal that as a small child he was lonely and took small steps to reduce the pain with a symptom companion. Over the years, if the loneliness continued, he nurtured this companion until it overshadowed the pain that initially caused him to embrace it.

An adult who is crazy, withdrawn, and hallucinatory did not choose this behavior out of the clear blue sky. He began developing it years before with short periods of voluntary detachment, withdrawal, and involvement with his own thoughts. His symptoms were kept under control until a severe stress, an extreme rejection, or a long period of loneliness and failure occurred, causing him to grasp and elaborate his previous mild symptoms into a complete withdrawal from reality, a withdrawal we call psychosis.

No symptom that people use, even as small children of five or six, much less as adults, is chosen without reason. It is normal for children to choose to create an imaginary companion, as Christopher Robin created Winnie-the-Pooh. Children will not suffer loneliness when they can easily conjure up a friend. Later, as children grow and mature, they learn that a certain amount of loneliness and rejection is part of life and, as Elwood P. Dowd discovered when he embraced Harvey, that adults around them are intolerant of any continued association with imaginary companions. Children dispense with imaginary companions or withdrawal into their own thoughts as long as they have involvement or are confident they will have it. If, as children, they withdrew into their own thoughts frequently and successfully, later, as adults, they may withdraw into psychosis should they suffer a period of severe loneliness.

Psychosis is rarely understood as a choice by either the adult who adopts it or by the people who are involved with him: his doctor, family, employer, or friends. If anyone involved with him suspects that the psychosis is indeed a choice, he finds it difficult to say so. Voicing such a suspicion makes everyone uncomfortable because everyone then has or might believe he has some responsibility for not relieving the loneliness that caused the patient to choose psychosis. It is much easier for everyone to believe that the person just got "sick" and that no one has any responsibility for what happened. In addition we do not like to admit that craziness is a choice because we are all a little crazy at times; if we admit that it is a choice for others, we must also admit it as a choice for ourselves. The patient will not admit he has made a choice because he would then see that both his previous lonely life and his present crazy life are self-created. His symptoms are of course specifically chosen to help him avoid such an under-standing. The doctor will not admit it is a choice because he would then have to admit that mental illness as a disease is only a scientific fantasy. Such an admission would conflict with his omnipotent healing role—a doctor cannot heal crazi-ness as he can appendicitis or streptococcus sore throat.

To begin helping this patient, the doctor must foster a mu-tual involvement strong enough to cause the patient to choose the doctor's companionship over the symptom's companion-ship. A doctor's belief in himself as a healer and his "knowl-edge" of the "science of mental illness" conflict with the idea of mutual involvement; the fact that the patient needs him, not his science or his medication, reduces his own medical self-esteem. Many doctors, therefore, refusing to believe that patients choose symptoms, become upset and incensed when confronted with evidence that patients do. For example, when doctors discover that what appears to be a mysterious skin dis-ease is only a series of self-inflicted cigarette burns, they become angry because they cannot comprehend how someone can choose such an odd companion. The only way most doc-tors can accept such behavior is to deny the symptom is chosen and label it mental illness. In doing so, they hinder the pa-tient from getting the help he needs.

As with psychosis, other psychological symptoms such as depressions, obsessions, compulsions, manias, and phobias are first learned and then chosen. At first, the person tests the symptom gingerly, or he sees it used successfully by someone else; sometimes both occur. Later, looking for a way to escape the pain of loneliness, to avoid facing his incompetence and inadequacy in becoming involved and worthwhile, he em-braces the learned symptom to reduce the pain as much as possible.

Traditional psychiatry avoids dealing with the present by delving into the past to discover when the patient first experienced failure and loneliness. The Oedipus complex, rich in psychological traditions, which many patients have painstakingly explored in traditional psychotherapy, is probably valid to the extent that there is indeed a time when a well-nurtured infant discovers that his mother has other important involvements besides him. The discovery forces him to abandon his belief that he is the center of all involvement. Most small children learn to adjust to the periods when mother is busy with father (or brother, sister, and others) and develop the competence to give as well as to take.

Contrary to Freud's interpretation of the fantasies of his wealthy patients living in a sexually repressive society, a small boy does not desire his mother sexually. He wants her total attention and resents the interference of his father or anyone else. If the child has a kind and loving father and a realistic, nonenveloping mother who does not use him as a wedge for her husband's attention, this period is weathered easily. If he later spends years in therapy finding out that he, as everyone else, had some loneliness and rejection when young, he has not only wasted time but has also harmed himself. Such a search is harmful because it almost always becomes an end in itself, an intellectual involvement that precludes the lonely person from doing now what he should be doing in the real world: learning to become successfully involved with others. To avoid the issue of present behavior by searching for remote periods of loneliness or for rejections early in life when the symptom was learned is wrong. The wrong is compounded by excusing a patient's lonely, incompetent involvement with his symptom by labeling the symptom an illness. These three errors—encouraging the patient to blot out the present, excusing the patient's involvement with his symptom, and labeling his symptom as an illness—relieve the patient from the responsibility of learning successful involvement with others, of facing his loneliness and failure, and of admitting that his symptom is his own choice.

Of the companions commonly chosen as pain relievers, alcohol merits special discussion because of its destructive and debilitating effect on literally millions of people. When the companionship of alcohol becomes so intense that it dominates the person, the person is an alcoholic. Its importance is recognized no matter what category—crime, disease, or behavior problem—it is put into. The law considers drunkenness a crime and jails the alcoholic. Many people, seeing how ineffective it is to put an alcoholic in jail for a few hours or a few days, have correctly tried to remove plain drunkenness from the list of criminal offenses. Their approach, unfortunately, is to call alcoholism a disease. The chairman of a United States Senate subcommittee, himself an ex-alcoholic, testified that alcoholism ranks third among killing sicknesses in the United States, outranked only by heart disease and cancer. He added, "There is an important difference. Everyone knows that cancer and heart trouble are diseases. Far too many people persist in regarding alcoholism as a behavior problem rather than an illness that is often fatal."

Although the Senator is helpful in pointing out the importance of alcoholism and by not discussing it as a crime, by calling alcoholism a disease and thus implying that it can be "cured" by a medical procedure, he denies the alcoholic and many who would help him the understanding that human involvement is needed. Told that he is sick and not responsible for his failing behavior, the alcoholic will not give up the companion that relieves his loneliness.

Physical symptoms such as stomach ulcer or colitis, asthma or chronic back pain, headaches or eczema are less clear-cut as choices. Yet these symptoms, commonly called psychosomatic symptoms, serve as well as or better than psychological symptoms as companions. Does a person choose these symptoms in the same way he chooses to be crazy or depressed? Although we do not know, it does not affect how we treat the person whether the symptom was created as a companion or whether, once established, it was then selected as a companion. Once present it effectively provides companionship for failure. For example, there is some evidence that stomach ulcers are common in children as well as in adults; adults who as children had stomach ulcers will probably choose the same symptom when confronted with loneliness and failure. There may be a constitutional weakness or an organic predisposition in the genetic structure for some people to have a particular psychosomatic symptom. Another possibility is that a child's mother may overemphasize one part of his body, such as his digestive system, his bowel movements, his skin, or his respiratory system, to the extent that he begins to value excessively one part of his body and to use it as a companion under stress.

Once a symptom such as ulcer, asthma, colitis, or migraine headache is established, many secondary involvements become possible. A faithful ulcer will gain a doctor's attention, easy access to drugs to relieve the suffering, and fashionable acceptance by others who have or respect ulcers. Because of the intense publicity given to illness, more people choose involvement with an illness today than in earlier times when sickness was less discussed. Also, psychosomatic illness is at present more stylish and thus more acceptable to others than are psychological symptoms.

Some doctors understand the role of the ulcer as a companion. They do not, however, say to a patient, "You're only suffering from a stomach ulcer to get sympathy, to get attention, and as a last-resort companion. If you reduce your work and become responsibly involved with more people, your ulcer will go away." Saying this would do no good and might lead to a worsening of the symptom by making the patient feel more rejected. An understanding doctor does not lecture the patient because he knows that the patient needs more than a lecture; he needs involvement. The doctor unfortunately has no time to get involved with the patient and no plan to help the patient find involvement with others. Able to offer only medical treatment, the doctor ignores or avoids the social issue. Unless the patient is acutely ill, he does not need medicine, X-rays, and continuous checkups and lab tests, but kind and firm encouragement to examine his present life carefully and find more responsible involvement with others. The entire treatment—the trips to the doctor, the tests, the hospitalization, the medication, the clinic visits, the opinions of medical consultants—becomes a secondary involvement that reinforces the value of the psychosomatic symptom as a companion and precludes the patient's learning more responsible ways to handle his life than being sick.

It is notable that even a disease caused by a biologic agent, such as a pneumococcal pneumonia, can serve the same purpose for a failing person. It can quickly become a companion and even replace his usual, long-term choice of symptoms for a time. When I was working in a mental hospital as a young resident there was a patient who was extremely hostile. Every time I offered to shake his hand, he would spit on the floor, curse me, and loudly accuse me of persecuting him. He would usually refuse to look at me, and both of us were uncomfortable when we were close to each other. One day, instead of his usual behavior, he asked me, warmly and clearly, whether he could see me privately after I finished making rounds. When we went into my office, he said that he did not feel well, that he had a back pain and a cough, and that he thought he had a fever. Saying this reasonably with no trace of his previous attitude, he asked me to examine him. I did and found that he was suffering from lobar pneumonia. I sent him to the hospital ward where acutely ill patients were treated. When I visited him there, he was kind to me and he thanked me continually for my help. He did not show any of his psychotic symptoms. As he recovered, his crazy behavior slowly returned. Although most of his symptoms came back, he no longer rejected me. He always shook my hand and thanked me for coming to see him each morning on my rounds. He had taken me, but no one else, into his world.

Perhaps today, with more experience, I could have used our small involvement as a start toward greater involvement. At the time, I was unsuccessful; when I left the hospital, he was there and now, twenty years later, he probably is still there. Certainly he did not choose to catch pneumonia. When he did, however, he was able to substitute this organic illness, a pressing, externally caused, dangerous symptom, for a previously chosen psychological symptom. There is good evidence that patients in mental hospitals have few psychosomatic diseases. They are unnecessary because the patients have a strong companion in their craziness.

Among the indigent are many lonely and failing people with a wide variety of "medical" problems. The whole county hospital routine becomes a way of life for them. Long waits for treatment, additional waiting for drugs, shuffling from one clinic to another, and receiving a variety of kind and callous treatment all serve to reinforce their involvement with their sickness. Even if the county hospitals suddenly became efficient and treated all patients with quick, sterile effectiveness for their symptoms, the patient load would not diminish. As long as the patients remain failures, they will search for and find new complaints to provide involvement, an involvement presently partially supplied by the lack of efficiency of the county hospital system. It will be impossible to provide efficient and impersonal government-financed symptomatic medical help for all those who complain.

We need a society that provides people with a chance to succeed, a chance for involvement, a chance to do something worthwhile. We need such a society far more than we need hospitals, clinics, and scientific medicine that are not applicable to the problems of failing people. If we keep expanding our traditional medical services in an attempt to treat failures who are not organically ill, we will be overwhelmed with the expense of these useless procedures. We must develop methods to screen the organically ill who are essentially successful from two groups: first, the organically ill who are failures, those whose organic illness may rapidly take on a companion role and continue long past its bodily cure; and second, those who develop psychosomatic illnesses as failure companions. A method of accomplishing the screening is suggested by Dr. Sidney R. Garfield in the April 1970 issue of *Scientific American*. In this excellent article Dr. Garfield also suggests that a major flaw of current medical practice is the excessive time spent trying to find something wrong with healthy people by applying the techniques taught for diagnosing illness.

Antisocial, often delinquent, aggressive, hostile behavior that separates us from other people is another kind of companionship often chosen by people who fail. A person who is involved with a depression may hope that others who are aware of his misery will try to reach him. He may rebuff those who try but, at the same time, hope they will try again. Other psychological symptoms, as well as medical symptoms, can be used similarly by a failing person to reach others, although if he holds too tightly to these symptoms he will probably drive away those who wish to help him.

Antisocial or hostile behavior, however, rarely serves to bring others closer to the failing person. People who might help tend to give up quickly, especially if the behavior is extreme because, unlike psychological and medical companions, the choice factor is obvious. No one believes that anger, scheming, cheating, or crime is a disease. The burden of change is clearly on the person who acts in an antisocial manner. Our legal structure is based on the premise that a person who commits a crime knows what he is doing. His behavior is a conscious choice. Legal excuses exist for criminal behavior that is claimed to be a product of mental illness or of an irresistible impulse. Well-meaning though ill-advised efforts are continually made to enlarge the categories of legal excuses. These efforts are based on the idea that a person should not be punished for his symptoms, criminal or otherwise, an idea with which I agree. I believe in addition, however, that he should not be excused. A better alternative for dealing with criminal behavior than either giving punishment or accepting excuses is discussed in Chapters Nine and Ten.

People who identify themselves as failures often have no emotional or psychosomatic symptoms. They have learned to reduce their pain by behaving, by acting, in certain ways that usually gain them attention or recognition, but serve to reinforce their failure identity. Failing schoolchildren are often antisocial, hostile, and difficult to teach because their behavior is in direct opposition to the work of school. Almost all juvenile delinquents and a high percentage of adult criminals are and were school failures. Swindling, promiscuity, hatemongering, and spreading sadomasochistic pornographic literature are additional examples of the behavior of failures who prey upon people. A failure with a predatory behavioral companion is characterized by an absence of social responsibility and a desire for immediate gratification of his wants. Isolated from others, totally involved with his own actions, and greedy to satisfy his own desires, he has no concern for how his behavior affects society because he perceives others only as objects to be manipulated and exploited. Although some failures who prey on others are charming and sociable, their behavior is never honest. They feign interest in other people because they have learned it is the best and quickest way to get what they want. Literature has many charming scoundrels, such as Billy Bigelow in *Carousel*, and real life also has no shortage of them.

Few people involved with antisocial behavior are as attractive as Billy Bigelow. Displaying instead a typical delinquent pattern, they start early in life to get into trouble because of school failure and its attendant social rejection. Feeling failure, the person chooses behavior that gains attention from others, regardless of any rules. Although the negative attention he gets reinforces his failure, it still provides some satisfaction because, having long since given up any idea that he can succeed in school, he still needs recognition to fulfill his need to be involved. Believing that normal pathways of involvement are closed, he struggles to attract attention. The best way that he sees is to disrupt the school and the community. This always gets attention.

Also characteristic of failures involved with their own antagonistic behavior is their development of a style—a slang language, a way to wear their hair, and a particular kind of clothes—designed to call attention to their chosen behavior. Advertising what they are capable of doing is important to them. The Hell's Angels, a motorcycle group whose members flaunt their capabilities, do not always behave antisocially, but they believe it is important that people know they can. The self-involvement of antisocial failures is characterized by thoughtless, spur-of-the-moment action and little concern for either their own or other people's safety. It is as if their attention-getting behavior were more important to them than their own selves. Knives, guns, tire chains, and broken bottles are commonly used in fights by people involved with their own hostile behavior.

As a depressed man's companion is his depression, so is a delinquent man's companion his behavior. Often as stereotyped and consistent as that of a compulsive hand-washer, his behavior confirms his failure and locks him into a position in which he is treated with hostility. He has little conscious appreciation for what he is doing that causes others to treat him negatively because his involvement with a delinquent style of life prevents him from becoming involved with others. Estranged and lonely, delinquents rationalize that being warm, kind, and caring for other people is a sign of weakness.

Almost all the relationships that antagonistic, hostile people attempt are characterized by quick boredom. Although they may form dramatic and overwhelming attachments, they are usually short-lived because each has little emotionally and nothing intellectually to give the other person. Often they victimize others sexually, and their quick, intense, often frenetic physical activity peaks and cools, repeating itself in a consistently erratic pattern that provides nothing upon which to build a relationship. Always seeking excitement, they prowl constantly looking for a situation in which their hostile behavior is appropriate. They are so involved with their companion that everything they say, think, or plan is a rationalization for their all-important behavior. They believe that the world is against them, that people are no good, that honesty and hard work are for suckers, and that the road is too long and the path is too steep. When arrested, they beg for another chance because in custody they are unable to behave as they want. Separated from their faithful companion by jail, they will do anything for a chance to rejoin it. They will promise anything, but because they have no involvement, promises and commitments are meaningless to them.

In terms of power or money, not all people involved with predatory companions are failures. Their single-minded devotion to what they do, their complete disregard for the feelings and the rights of others, and their ability to become involved with people only as they can exploit them may help these people gain power and wealth. Harry Brock, the scrap dealer in *Born Yesterday*, epitomized such an individual in a struggle for wealth. Hitler, Stalin, and Mussolini are examples of leaders seeking power rather than wealth.

A few lonely people who never gain human involvement, love, or respect do succeed in gaining wealth or power through their total disregard for others and their total involvement with their own behavior. For each one who succeeds, however, thousands of others fail. Involved with their hostile behavior and without wealth or power, they lead a life of misery, frequently becoming alcoholics or drug addicts to reduce their pain. We help these people in the same way that we help others who are involved with an idea, a symptom, or an emotion. We must become involved with them and give them the initial experience of a warm, human relationship. Difficult as this is to do in the cases discussed earlier, it is even more difficult to do in cases of hostile behavior because such people's hostility directly prevents involvement. Because their hostility immediately focuses on whoever attempts to approach them, breaking through their wall and becoming involved requires great skill.

A particular kind of involvement with one's own behavior is exhibited by a person who behaves violently and rationalizes what he does on the basis of political alienation. Evaluating his actions as an attempt to call attention to an oppressive government that does not allow him and others freedom to fulfill their social needs, he believes force, hostility, aggression, and anger are necessary to bolster his efforts and to get others to join him in working for radical changes. Few in number, these people are considered newsworthy, and therefore the media tend to magnify their importance.

In addition to failures trying to change the political and social system, many successful people, people with warm, worthwhile involvements, work hard toward various political and philosophical goals. They also claim our present system has serious flaws, and they are willing to use some force, not to overthrow the government, but to call attention to their beliefs and to the need for change. They say that the flaws are those goal-oriented government policies that are in direct opposition to helping people become successful because they do not provide the pathways to responsible involvement that we need. Both groups condemn the draft, expenditures for higher armaments, racial discrimination, drug laws, and all laws that regulate a person's behavior if that behavior harms no one else.

The difference in motivation between these two groups, whose aims seem similar, is great. Those in the first group are motivated by failure and have become obsessively involved with their own behavior. Those in the second group are generally involved and successful. They believe in, and are motivated by, not their involvement with their own behavior but rather their compassion for others and their frustration when they see so many people lonely and failing in this society that is technically and, I believe, socially capable of providing many more pathways to success than it does. Those in the second group must not let their compassion for others allow them to embrace hostile and destructive behavior. In their zeal to help, they must learn not to cooperate with those who claim political alienation but who are really using this claim only to excuse their hostile, antisocial acts. It is tempting to associate with people who seem almost careless of their own lives because they do gain attention, yet their very disregard of their own lives and the lives of others is antithetical to the changes they are trying to make.

Our society cannot differentiate between the members of these two groups when a person commits a crime; all must be treated equally by the law. We must not, however, make honest protesters into lawbreakers by passing laws that prevent them from protesting nonviolently. In addition, we need disciplined and sensitive police who do not indiscriminately arrest all who protest, whether or not they are breaking a law. Unless we are careful on these two points, we will close pathways for honest political action and force those who might be successful into the role of failure by giving them no peaceful options to express their concern for their fellow man.

If we are going to move into a more human identity society, we will not do so through the use of force. The concepts of

Martin Luther King and Gandhi are geared to the identity society. The survival power concepts of Mao, Franco, Castro, and Idi Amin of Uganda are not. Cesar Chavez, by getting concerned citizens to boycott grapes and by avoiding a direct confrontation with the growers and with police, is a living demonstration that organization, cooperation, and patient self-sacrifice will bring about effective change in the identity society.

Therefore, all symptoms, psychological or psychosomatic, and all hostile, aggressive, irrational behavior are products of loneliness and personal failure. They are companions to the lonely, failing, suffering people who, struggling for an identity, do not succeed and who identify themselves as failures. The failure is focused onto a symptom companion to reduce the pain of loneliness. When the symptom companion itself is painful, a further attempt is made to reduce the pain with drugs and alcohol. In our role-dominated society the more we have people who identify themselves as failures, the more they will become involved with failure companions.

Chapter Four

Reality Therapy

Reality Therapy is a way to gain and to maintain a successful identity. In the book *Reality Therapy* I describe its use with people whom I then called irresponsible and whom I now also call people with failure identities. These same principles are also briefly discussed in *Schools Without Failure* as a basis for helping a failing child gain success in school. The principles of Reality Therapy need not be restricted to professionals helping irresponsible people or to teachers helping failing children gain successful identities. On the contrary, these principles may be used by anyone—parents, ministers, doctors, husbands, and wives—wishing to gain and to help others gain and maintain successful identities. The more people able to gain successful identities, the more successful the identity society will be. The society will founder if too many people cannot become successful, cannot gain the involvement and the confidence that they are competent and worthwhile, loved and loving.

In the survival society people also strove for a successful

identity, but its achievement was less in personal fulfillment than in achieving security. Now, in the identity society, a successful identity is possible for a half-billion people. It is incumbent upon successful people to help and teach others to become successful and to show and convince them that pathways to success and involvement do exist in our new society. We have seen enough turmoil in the first twenty-five years of the identity society to recognize the drain on the society and the potential for trouble caused by those who identify themselves as failures.

Reality Therapy is not exclusively for the "mentally ill," incompetent, disturbed, or emotionally upset. It is a system of ideas designed to help those who identify with failure learn to gain a successful identity and to help those already successful to maintain their competence and help others become successful.

The test of any practice, therapy, or series of therapeutic concepts designed to help people succeed is whether or not it works. After fifteen years of using the principles of Reality Therapy and teaching them to others, I contend that they do work and that their application can be taught to competent people who wish to use them. These principles are clear, they are explained without jargon, and they are applicable to any failure, whether it is long-lasting and deeply seated or short-term and lightly rooted. Obviously, psychiatrists and psychologists who work with seriously failing people need extensive training and deep commitment to use Reality Therapy consistently for long periods. The same degree of training and commitment is unnecessary for laymen; however, the better anyone understands the principles, the more success he will experience when he applies them. The principles of Reality Therapy may be used by parents with children, teachers with students, ministers with parishioners, and employers with employees. One of the best ways to gain a successful identity for oneself is to use these principles in everyday life; as you try to live a better and happier life yourself, you will help those around you.

That these ideas can be used by laymen in no way lessens the value or makes less professional a therapist who uses them. The professional differs from the layman because he elects to help people with strong identifications with failure who are beyond the competence of most nonprofessional people. The professional Reality Therapist does nothing different from anyone else using the same principles; when he helps a child, he does what that child's parents should have done earlier to prevent the child from identifying as a failure. Bringing a special tenacity to his work, the therapist has a commitment to stay involved and never give up. He develops a wide variety of involvement techniques because his ability to become involved is the basic ingredient of Reality Therapy. If he cannot successfully become involved, he will fail. He usually has more experience with the other principles as well; unless he can figure out how to become involved, however, the other principles cannot be applied successfully.

Involvement with at least one successful person is a requirement for growing up successfully, maintaining success, or changing from failure to success. Using his skill to become involved, the therapist helps toward success those whose friends and relations have inadequate skills to assist. They include the employee whose employer has given him up, the member of the congregation whose minister has counseled him without success, and the child whose parents have reached their wits' end. Accepting the responsibility to work with those who need his help, the therapist must make a constant effort to improve his skills, especially his skill to become involved. Although the practice of Reality Therapy is readily understandable, it is not easy to do. It takes skill and experience to apply these ideas successfully. In addition to the training he receives, the successful therapist must have warmth, strength, and confidence.

In the Veterans Administration Psychiatric Hospital in West Los Angeles, where I worked as a resident at the beginning of my career, we would often get patients who were completely crazy. When such a patient arrived, I would say to the chief ward attendant, a man of much experience and humanity but little formal training, "Mr. Bland, work with this new patient, get acquainted with him, and do what you always seem to be able to do so that by Monday he is settled down, no longer crazy, and I can talk with him." Over the weekend he talked with him and almost always made friends with him and became involved with him. The patient settled down, gave up his extreme craziness, and willingly discussed his situation on Monday morning when I returned to the ward. Mr. Bland was a superb Reality Therapist. He probably practiced this therapy as well as anyone who ever worked in a mental hospital. He had warmth, kindness, strength, and the desire to help people. Watching him and talking to him, I learned a great deal. Mr. Bland was not a professional therapist, and he later left the ward to take a higher-paying job in the Veterans Administration. However, whatever it is that professional people strive for in the practice of psychotherapy, Mr. Bland had it. The principles that he used, principles that I did not recognize then but now see so clearly, were the basic principles of Reality Therapy.

This and the next four chapters contain ideas that anyone who has found involvement and gained a success identity can learn to use to help maintain his success. The more a person is aware of these principles and makes an effort to use them, the better chance he has to gain greater success. The possibility also exists that a person who has identified with failure, a person who lives haphazardly and then wonders why he has so little pleasure and so much pain, can read this chapter carefully and gain an understanding of how he must begin to behave to find success. To use these ideas successfully, however, will be much harder for him than for the already successful person.

As we have discussed, failures become involved with themselves and with symptoms or irresponsible behavior that cause them and those around them to suffer. By themselves, they cannot help themselves. As practiced both professionally and nonprofessionally, Reality Therapy is designed to help failing people become involved and to gain and then to maintain a successful identity. Reality Therapy does not always succeed. When it does not, it is usually because whoever is helping is unable to get involved in a meaningful, long-term way with the person who is failing. In therapy, failure to get involved is not the fault of the person who is failing, although once he begins to become involved he must strive for greater involvement. If he does not, he shares responsibility for his continued failure. The therapist, however, must begin the involvement.

In life, it is a family responsibility for parents and children to stay involved with each other, but the parents must take the lead. It is a minister's responsibility to keep involved with his congregation, but it is the parishioner's responsibility to seek and to support the minister and help him to be successful. A good employer is responsible for involvement with his employees, as is a good teacher with her students. In marriage, usually either the husband or the wife accepts the primary responsibility to keep the involvement going at any one time.

When a marriage fails, when a child is unsuccessful, when a student is irresponsible, when a business fails because the employees are unmotivated, the failure usually starts as involvement begins to break down. There is then less and less chance for responsible behavior. Involvement alone does not lead to success, as many disappointed people have discovered who became involved in sensitivity groups, and later found their lives unchanged, but involvement is necessary as a prerequisite to success.

Based upon successful involvement, the principles of Reality Therapy evolve into an approach to life that can help a person become successful or, at least, understand his failure and try another direction. Our options are almost never closed; we just believe they are. Many options exist in the identity society for people who wish to find success by living according to these principles. In discussing the principles of Reality Therapy, I will show their application by laymen in the situations of everyday life, as well as their application by professionals to people with serious failure identities.

The Principles of Reality Therapy

The principles of Reality Therapy are described in the order in which they are usually applied. Although the order may sometimes vary and there is always some overlap, I believe this order makes the principles most readily understandable. I have tried to make the descriptions complete enough and to include enough examples in this and the following chapters so that anyone can begin to apply Reality Therapy. Each person will then, as he gains experience, develop a technique congenial to him and appropriate to the people and the situations with which he is dealing.

1. INVOLVEMENT. Basic to man is the need for involve-

ment. For Reality Therapy to work, the therapist or helper must become involved with the person he is trying to help; the therapist, therefore, must be warm, personal, and friendly. No one can break the intense self-involvement of failure by being aloof, impersonal, or emotionally distant. Warmth and understanding are needed for the two people to become initially involved, if they are professional therapist and patient, or reinvolved, if they are a husband and wife or a parent and child. Whatever time it takes, someone must break through the loneliness and the self-involvement to start a warm, intimate, emotional involvement where little or none existed before. Without warm emotional involvement there is no possibility of success in working with a difficult, lonely patient or a failing child. Involvement is necessary for everyone; it is a prerequisite for a successful person to maintain his success identity, for a student to learn, for an employee to do well and earn a promotion. Whether you seek help for failure or for becoming more successful, if you do not feel that you are warmly and personally accepted by the person who is helping you, your chance of becoming successful is small.

Involvement is the foundation of therapy. All other principles build on and add to it. As soon as possible, the person being helped must begin to understand that there is more to life than being involved with his misery, symptoms, obsessive thoughts, or irresponsible behavior. He must see that another human being cares for him and is willing to discuss his life and talk about anything both consider worthwhile and interesting. In this relationship any subject of mutual interest can serve as a bridge to build involvement. Any subject can provide the warmth and give-and-take that help a failing person learn that he can be accepted by and accepting of another human being.

A problem of the formal patient-therapist relationship is to establish this warmth and friendship with someone who needs involvement desperately, as most patients do, yet limit the involvement to what is possible in the situation. To an involved person, the deliberate involvement of the professional therapist may seem to make therapy artificial, but to any uninvolved lonely person, warm friendly acceptance is not artificial. The therapist's problem is to provide enough involvement himself to help the patient develop confidence to make new, deep, lasting involvements of his own. It is not possible for a therapist, who is attempting to lead a responsible life of his own, to become deeply involved in time-consuming friendships with everyone who comes to him for help. Among friends or family, where there is no specific time limitation, the involvement can proceed as far as each person desires.

The helping person, whether friend, family member, or professional therapist, must be honest and never promise to give more time than he plans to give. Even patients who desperately need their therapist will, upon becoming involved, accept an honest statement from the therapist that he can give only a specific amount of time. The therapist should point out that, nevertheless, the patient has much more time with a person with whom he is involved than he had before. To weather this common crisis is a skill that a good therapist learns. It is difficult to tell a starving man that he can have only a little food when he believes there is so much more. The therapist's job is to convince the patient that he has chosen starvation and that there is plenty of food around if he will go out and look for it; the therapist is not the only one with food. The skilled therapist becomes enough involved with the patient in the hour or two a week they spend together to help the patient gain confidence that he can develop involvement with others. An advantage of group therapy is that each person becomes involved with people other than the therapist and thus can more easily develop involvements outside the therapy situation.

Although the therapist has little time, it does not mean that he cannot have a big impact. The time with the patient is devoted exclusively to him. Although at first glance an hour a week may not seem like a lot of personal attention, it is. Many people, husband and wife, parent and child, in their ordinary busy lives do not get more than an hour a week of warm, exclusive time with someone with the skill of using this time to get involved. A suggestion I make to many parents having difficulty with a child is to devote an hour a week— the hour a week I would give to the child if he saw me—just to the child, doing what he wants to do. Although following this suggestion usually helps the child greatly, it is disheartening how many parents refuse to make this seemingly simple effort.

In the relationship anything is open for discussion, a difficult concept for patients and beginning therapists to understand, but natural and easy for friends or family to accept. It is unwise to talk at length about a patient's problems or his misery. Some of my most successful cases have been people who quickly got the idea that there was much more to life than their immediate problems. They discussed much that interested us both, even some of what I was doing. Current news, movies, books, plays, aspirations, personal relations, and family are all good grist for involvement and can help people become more involved. The patient's problems seldom enter into many of the therapy hours. Interesting nonproblem discussions valuable in therapy because they serve to build involvement are common to good conversation between friends, husbands and wives, parents and children, teachers and students, ministers and congregation. The discussions develop the intellectual sharing that is important in Reality Therapy. They should be challenging, with values, opinions, and beliefs brought out and some emotion generated.

Talking at length about a patient's problems and his feelings about them focuses upon his self-involvement and consequently gives his failure value. Long discussions about the patient's problems are a common and serious error in psychotherapy. They increase rather than decrease his self-involvement and his misery. For example, a patient may come to me because he is depressed and feels valueless and unwanted. The less we talk about his depression, drug taking, and suicidal gestures and the more we discuss the possibilities that are open to him, the better he feels. It is tempting to listen to his complaints because they seem so urgent. Doing so may reduce his pain and make him feel better for a while as he basks in the attention his complaints have gained him. If he does nothing to change his behavior, however, his pain will return and he will grow disillusioned with therapy. Also, to gain continued attention, he may behave more and more irresponsibly so that he has something valid to complain about. If we then listen with renewed interest, we only compound the error. Later, when we try to discuss other subjects, he will resist because he had been getting his failure reinforced and his pain temporarily reduced with each new complaint that was heard.

Many people who enter into therapy with a Reality Therapist are surprised when they find themselves talking about and enjoying a wide variety of subjects. They say, "Well, I certainly feel better and I function better, but I wonder if I should be talking about these nonessentials instead of my own particular deep and serious problems." Keeping the conversation warm and focused away from the patient's problems, the therapist can reassure the patient that these discussions are worthwhile. Although the therapist can, if necessary, explain why the talks are worthwhile, it is better if he need not do so. It is preferable to conduct therapy so that the patient himself sees value in the talks. Explaining why the discussions are important is like telling a person why you like him; it is better and more satisfying if you can demonstrate it. Patients with the traditional therapy experience of talking continually about themselves and their incompetence need a long time to understand Reality Therapy's emphasis on warm, involving conversations rather than direct concern with the patient's problems.

Between friends and in well-run groups, conversation on many subjects naturally occurs. The worst thing anyone can do for a depressed friend is to let him whine excessively about his troubles. Instead, good friends say, "Come on, let's do something now. Let's talk about something besides you. Let's forget our concerns and enjoy talking." They know that they cannot solve their friend's problems by listening to complaints. A therapist must never give the impression that he has the power to change a patient's life once he is aware of the patient's problem. What the therapist does is not parallel to common medical practice. He can never prescribe and cure as the doctor often can. Rather, the relationship that makes good friendships should guide therapy. People who have not had previous therapy usually do not question the Reality Therapy approach, and they do not try to focus on their problems. Those who have had prior therapy, after being in Reality Therapy for a while, begin to understand how it differs. They accept it because they feel better. With little talk about a person's problems, symptoms, and misery, Reality Therapy helps a person plan for and identify with success.

The therapist must also counteract a common reaction of lonely people with failure identities: running from anyone who tries to become involved with them. They interpret their lonely experience as being the fault of others who have rejected them rather than their own choice. In truth, they have rarely given others the opportunity for involvement with them, nor have they extended themselves to gain the friendship of others. Consequently, as I have described in Chapter Three, to reduce the pain they settle for themselves. When they begin to get involved with a therapist or anyone else, they must concern themselves about losing their faithful friend—their symptom or their irresponsible behavior. Seeing the therapist and perhaps others as threats to their self-involvement, they become worried because they know their old misery has always been so faithful and they doubt the wisdom of giving it up. The therapist's warm, personal involvement helps the patient understand that a person can replace the constant companionship of misery.

Talking enjoyably about worthwhile subjects is the best way to help oneself get involved. No one can gain a success identity alone. Trying to help others, if only through warm, enjoyable conversations, is the best way one can help oneself. From talking, people begin doing things together, and each helps the other by means of the involvement. Self-help requires getting involved with someone else; it can't be done at home alone like exercise.

2. CURRENT BEHAVIOR. No one can work to gain a successful identity or to increase his success without being aware of his current behavior. If a person denies his behavior or claims

to be unaware of it, he will be unable to gain or to maintain a successful identity. Whether the situation is a psychiatrist dealing with a psychiatric patient, a parent with a failing child, a teacher with a failing student, or any other situation in which one person tries to help another to live his life more successfully, success will come only if the person being helped is aware of what he is doing now. Accompanying the consistent warmth and involvement discussed in Principle One is constant effort by the therapist to help the patient become aware, consciously and in detail, of his own behavior at the present time. Examining current behavior is usually done matter-of-factly, although sometimes the therapist must work slowly and subtly. Because a patient may run from therapy when he becomes aware of what he is doing, the therapist must judge the strength of the involvement as he helps the patient become aware of his irresponsibility.

People often avoid facing their present behavior by emphasizing how they feel rather than what they are doing. Although Reality Therapy does not deny that emotions are important, successful therapists learn that unless they focus on behavior they do not help the patient. A man may say, "I know what I'm doing, but that is not important; what is important is how I feel." The therapist must respond by telling him that he accepts his feelings and that he believes that the patient is suffering. The therapist must not focus on feelings, however, because he knows it is almost impossible for a person to change his feelings significantly without first changing his behavior.

Neither in doing Reality Therapy, nor in raising children, nor in relating husband to wife, nor in any other relationship are feelings unimportant. Nevertheless, for a relationship to be successful, how we behave toward others is crucial. If we behave toward them in a competent, responsible way, we will eventually, if not immediately, feel good. If we attempt to relieve our pain by getting drunk when we feel lonely, we may experience the immediate good feelings that occur when we relieve the pain. But we will soon feel bad again and be tempted to get drunk again. If a child is having a tantrum and we attempt to soothe his feelings and stop his crying by promising whatever he wants, he may learn only to respond with a tantrum when frustrated. We fail the child because he does not learn to relieve his own frustrations.

A person often comes to my office complaining of how bad she feels. She is depressed, upset, worried, and miserable. Believing she should tell me about these feelings in great detail (in fact, she wants to), she is surprised when I, a psychiatrist, a person supposed to be keenly attuned to misery, cut her rather short and say, "I believe you. You have convinced me that you are depressed and I appreciate that you are upset. But what are you doing?"

Although I am not always this blunt, I make a statement to this effect as soon as I can. In therapy I neither deny her feelings nor say they are wrong or unimportant. I accept them, but I let her know that they are less important than her behavior. Until the patient gets used to this approach, when I ask, "What are you doing?" while she is complaining of the pain, she often replies, "What do you mean?" She is telling me she believes that most of what she is "doing" is feeling bad. Wholly involved with her misery, she cannot believe I am naïve enough to think that she is doing anything other than suffering. Actually, she is doing, or not doing, much that continues to keep her in pain. Applying the second principle of Reality Therapy, I must get her behavior out on the table so she can become aware of it. Unless we become aware of our behavior, we cannot learn to behave more competently.

Identification of oneself as a failure leads to antagonism

and withdrawal, accompanied by pain. The resultant self-involvement, which is an effort to reduce the pain, ordinarily keeps the failure from moving toward others. We must help the patient exchange self-involvement for involvements with others, the first step toward success. To help the patient see his behavior and choose new behavior that will lead to involvement with others, we continually ask, "What are you doing? What are you doing now? What did you do yesterday? What did you do the day before yesterday? What did you do last week?" A week is about as far back as we should go if we see a person weekly. We need not go that far back when living with a person as a parent, husband, or wife.

In my office, I have often heard husbands and wives, together and separately, make a long series of complaints about the other's behavior. Each tells me how upset the other's behavior has made him feel and how destructive it is to the marriage. I ask, "I understand that you're having difficulty because of what your husband (wife) is doing and how it makes you feel, but what are *you* doing? Do you think *you* are doing anything destructive to the marriage?" These questions come as a complete surprise to many people. Not wanting to look at what they are doing, they hope the therapist will spend his time listening to their complaining about how grievously their mate misuses them. A parent trying to referee a fight between children who blame each other must ask similar questions. The parent who raises successful children asks one, "All right, what did *you* do to start the fight?" and asks the other, "What did *you* do to keep the fight going?"

No husband can change a wife's behavior without altering his own; no wife can change a husband's behavior by disregarding her own. Each must change his own behavior. Some marriage counseling neglects this vital point and, in doing so, may harm rather than help. Even in a case in which a husband is all wrong and his wife is behaving responsibly, she probably must change her behavior in some way to break the ice and motivate her husband to change his behavior.

When the girls from the Ventura School for Delinquent Girls went home, they often wrote me to say, "My mother has changed; she's so much nicer to me now than she used to be." They do not recognize—and sometimes they *do* recognize— that they are no longer running around, drinking, taking drugs, and staying out all night. They are going to school, perhaps holding a job, coming home, and keeping normal hours with different friends. Naturally, their behavior change has caused drastic changes in their parents' approach to them.

Thus in Reality Therapy, although we do not disregard feelings, we rarely ask people how they are feeling because we emphasize behavior. Neither do we use the common and simplistic therapy ploy of telling a patient, "You appear angry," or "You appear upset," or "What you are saying seems hostile to me." These statements lead to a detailed examination of present feelings, a discussion wrongly instigated by the therapist. These simple, noninvolving statements, traditionally taught in Psychiatry 101, are avoided in Reality Therapy because they emphasize and give value to self-involvement and to the emotions stemming from it. If a person is hostile, we accept his hostility, but we do not make an issue of it. We are trying to get him to learn to function regardless of his hostility.

Friends need not behave as therapists and emphasize behavior over feelings. Friends do not separate them. Even if one person is trying to help another, the friendship should develop naturally. When friends talk only about how they feel, however, the friendship becomes boring, especially if one friend is complaining all the time. In friendship (or in marriage) people must do things together. The best feelings arise from what people do together that they enjoy. A complaining person may at times stimulate his friend's normal concern and briefly deepen the involvement. If he continues to complain, however, and if the friend feels powerless to help, the interminable complaining will weaken or destroy the friendship. The friend who sticks it out through thick and thin, listening to all the complaints and perhaps putting up with irresponsible behavior, is often surprised when the complainer, having become more responsible, avoids him. Because in the mind of the complainer the friend is associated with events in his life he would like to forget, the friend is discarded because he was, in a sense, too good a friend.

The second principle of Reality Therapy is thus to make the person being helped become aware of his behavior and to understand that his behavior is a self-involvement that he chooses. No one forces him to behave as he does; it is his present choice. When we are closely, warmly, and personally involved with him and when he accepts what he is doing as his choice, we are ready to take the third step in Reality Therapy.

3. EVALUATING YOUR BEHAVIOR. The patient must now look at his behavior critically and judge it on the basis of whether or not it is his best choice. The Reality Therapist must ask him to judge his behavior on the basis of whether he believes it is good for him and good for the people he cares about or would like to care about. He must also ask him whether his behavior is socially acceptable in his community. For example, if he is depressed or afraid to fly or has an ulcer, what he does usually has little effect on the community, but if he pushes drugs in a high school, what he does significantly affects the community and he must consider community mores in making his judgment.

This principle is often misunderstood. Some people accept and others reject Reality Therapy because they misunderstand this principle. Both groups believe the Reality Therapist acts as a moralist, which he does not; he never tells anyone that what he is doing is wrong and that he must change. The therapist does not judge the behavior; he leads the patient to evaluate his own behavior through their involvement and by bringing the actual behavior out in the open. Sometimes there is no clear-cut choice, but the patient must still decide what to do. Occasionally, people seem to hurt someone by moving away from him to help themselves move toward more responsible companions. Although making such a choice is usually better for everyone than making no decision, it is hard to do. For example, a divorce may hurt a couple's children, at least temporarily, but unless either the husband or the wife is strong enough to make this choice, the conflict between them may become intolerable and hurt the children more than a separation will. Rather than standing by while a person settles for an ulcer or a backache and the subsequent trip to the hospital that delays the choice, Reality Therapy helps him choose between working to save the marriage or getting divorced. Either choice will allow everyone concerned a better chance for success than will prolonging a bad situation. Reality Therapy gives the individual a chance to examine the situation and urges him to come to a decision.

No one changes his behavior away from failure unless first he is involved with someone—a therapist, a friend, a relative, a teacher—who he feels is worthwhile and who can make him believe that changing behavior is possible. Second, he must understand what he is doing. Finally, he must be able to make a value judgment about his behavior that he can then act upon. When a person judges his behavior as incompetent or irresponsible, that is, it is hurting himself and others, he has established the basis for change.

I believe that any involved person can evaluate his behavior. A person can judge his behavior without the help of a therapist if he has involvement that gives him some success and does some honest self-evaluation. Husbands and wives, teachers and ministers, employers and parents can help those near them make value judgments. Whoever helps another, however, must be careful not to make judgments himself but rather to lead toward self-judgment. No one does anything at any time unless he believes: This behavior is the best I can choose now.

A person with a serious failure identity behaves in ways that reinforce his failure identity because he thinks: This is the best I can do for myself at this particular time; I can't do any better. In Reality Therapy, when we lead a person to evaluate his behavior, at first he may say, "Well, what I'm doing now is all I am able to do. I know it's not the best, but I just don't think I can change." As our involvement increases, however, and as we ask him to reevaluate what he is doing, he usually sees that better choices are available.

Just as a therapist asks a patient to evaluate his behavior, so a parent must ask a child or a teacher a pupil. I believe all of us should continually evaluate ourselves, but doing so is difficult; it is easier if someone helps. Self-evaluation usually cannot be made unless the person feels that the therapist, or someone else he respects, cares about him. Lonely people involved with failure find it almost impossible to make an honest self-judgment. Characteristic of a person with a success identity is his ability to judge honestly what he is doing in a wide context; he faces reality and decides how he might act differently whenever he faces a problem. The ability to make reasonable value judgments is fostered in the therapy hour.

The therapist does not intimate: I know better than you do what you should do with your life. Once the patient makes a judgment, the therapist may, and usually does, help him plan its implementation. The judgment "I ought to change" belongs to the patient, however.

For example, when an alcoholic patient drinks he has made the value judgment that he wants a drink right now, even though he may recognize that drinking is bad for him and that he may get in trouble if he drinks now. Nevertheless, he makes the value judgment that the drink is worth it, or he would not drink. Later, he can moan and become involved with all the trouble and emotional turmoil caused by his choice to drink: how he lost his job, his wife, his family, and everything he valued. The therapist is not fooled by his moanings, for it means little as long as he chooses to drink. If he stops drinking, then he may indeed complain. From his complaint, that life is tough without alcohol, he may be led to a better choice. No matter what he says or how much he complains, as long as he drinks, alcohol is his choice.

The therapist helps him understand that when he drank, he made a value judgment—the drink was worth more than anything else—and that he must examine his choice if he wants to change. To quit drinking, he must make a value judgment and stick to it, that alcohol is a bad choice. We find it much easier to make a talking decision than a doing decision. A friend of mine who worked with drug users for years quotes them as saying, "It's not talking the talk but walking the walk that counts." As the involvement grows, the patient gains enough confidence to make value judgments that he is willing to act on. No one is unable to make a value judgment, but for those unwilling to do so, nothing can be done in therapy.

Parents must similarly ask their children for value judgments. If a child is doing poorly in school, not studying and perhaps cutting, the parent should approach him and ask him to decide whether his behavior is the best for him. Because no parent is capable of being nonjudgmental, the child is in an atmosphere of judgment. The parent can, however, refrain from punishment and threats. He can ask the child, "What are you doing and does it help you?" If a parent can approach a child nonjudgmentally in behavior, if not in belief, the child can begin to believe that he is responsible for his actions and can decide whether he should change. The parent might add, following the next principle of Reality Therapy to be discussed, "If you decide what you're doing isn't working maybe I can help." Anyone trying to help another person must get him to evaluate his behavior because no one will change his behavior to make it more responsible and thus open the way to a successful identity unless he evaluates his behavior in the light of how it is helping him and those around him.

Whatever the morality or the laws of the society, we can rarely excuse our behavior because we do not agree with them. We must understand that we have to accept the consequences of our behavior if we defy the existing morality or existing laws. Guidance by a concerned person able to point out the realities of the society helps us recognize what we are doing. If a young man wanted to protest the Vietnam war by failing to report for induction, he knew his behavior was cause for arrest. It was his decision, and he should have prepared himself for jail. The same risk applies to smoking marijuana openly.

In my experience, most individuals who feel failure gain strength more readily by conforming to the ongoing morality and laws of society; later, when they are stronger and more successful they may wish to defy them. The job of the Reality Therapist, when discussing morality and law and the patient's role in society, is to bring out everything that he can about them relevant to the decision the patient must make. Then, if the patient chooses an action to protest the war that leads to jail, he has made a rational, not an emotional, decision.

4. PLANNING RESPONSIBLE BEHAVIOR. Once someone makes a value judgment, the person helping him must assist in developing realistic plans for action to follow the value judgment. Many people can examine their behavior and decide that it is not helping them, but they have no experience or background for planning a more successful life. They do not know how to plan for more responsible, more competent behavior. Parents and teachers, husbands and wives, employers and ministers, as well as therapists must help people plan their lives more successfully in accordance with their decisions.

Because planning requires knowledge of what options are available, a therapist who talks with many people making plans gains experience not available to the average person. As many problems revolve around family life, a therapist who is married and has children is usually better able to help plan than is a therapist whose life has not included marriage and children. Encouraging the person who needs the help to make most of the plan himself is part of the therapist's skill. The therapist sometimes puts the person in touch with someone else. I have sent patients to friends or associates of mine who have more experience in particular fields to help the patient work out a detailed plan.

Never make a plan that attempts too much, because it will usually fail and reinforce the already present failure. A failing person needs success, and he needs small individually successful steps to gain it. A student who has never studied should not plan to study one hour a night; at the start, fifteen minutes once or twice a week is more realistic and is still a big change from his present failing behavior. The plan should be ambitious enough so that some change, small though it may be, can be seen, yet not so grand that failure is likely. Little steps can be extended; it is much harder to cut back on big steps.

It is rarely impossible for the patient to make a plan once he has made a value judgment that his present behavior is bad. There are, however, times when no reasonable plan can be made. In those cases therapy can only create involvement that makes the person more comfortable rather than establish a basis for success. Prisoners with long-term prison sentences, for example, cannot plan for success. Prison psychologists have asked me, "Can Reality Therapy help prisoners with mandatory twenty-five-year sentences?" I do not think it can because, although they might judge their previous behavior as wrong, their options for a successful life are essentially closed; there are few Birdmen of Alcatraz.

In the next four chapters I present various plans for common problems in everyday life. An example here is for a child failing in school. A plan might be to sit in the front instead of the back of the class, to take notes, to study on a certain schedule, and to cultivate friends who are successful in class and study with them. This four-point plan to help a failing student almost always works if it is carried out.

Plans are not final. Usually many different plans can solve a problem. If one plan does not work, successive plans can be made until one is found that does. Being locked into one plan is similar to being locked into self-involvement. On the other hand, jumping from plan to plan as soon as a little stress is encountered is also bad. The therapist or helping person must develop skill in assisting the patient to evaluate the plan's feasibility. The therapist must be firm if the plan is judged feasible and flexible if it is not.

5. COMMITMENT. After a reasonable plan has been made, it must be carried out. To give the person greater motivation to fulfill the plan, we ask him for a commitment to us. The commitment may be verbal or written; it may be given to an individual or to a group. It can be made between husband and wife, parent and child, teacher and student, therapist and patient. Commitment intensifies and accelerates the trying of new behavior. Without commitment, without warm human desire to say, "I'll do it for you as well as for me," plans are less likely to be implemented. Some people believe that commitment means dependence, that people should be self-motivated. A debate on the theoretical merits of self-motivation is useless, however, because many people need involvement at the point of change. Nothing is wrong with trying new behavior partly for someone else; we cannot live our lives alone successfully. Commitment to do something worthwhile for the sake of oneself and someone else is a natural outgrowth of the involvement necessary for success. Successful people seem to commit themselves on their own; they really commit themselves to everyone they are involved with. Failures, however, to get a plan started, need to make definite commitments to one person or a few people toward whom they are moving.

Characteristic of people with failure identities is their unwillingness to commit themselves because in their loneliness they do not believe that anyone cares what they do. In addition, they fear that if they commit themselves and fail, as they expect, they expose themselves to painful rejection. They may rationalize and excuse their failure, but it still hurts, and to them it is still failure. When failures actually make a commitment, they have, in poker parlance, tipped their hand and they know their bluff will be called. To a failure holding low cards, commitment is a dangerous play.

Commitment means commitment to the involvement. It verifies that the person to whom I commit myself is involved with me; thus I will do what we have planned because we are involved. Commitment binds the involvement. If friends make a date to go somewhere together, a commitment is implicit. If someone continually fails his commitments, he will soon cease to have any friends. His only commitment is to himself and his self-involvement. In Reality Therapy we help people who rarely keep commitments to others to do so. Until they do, they have little chance to gain a successful identity.

A commitment is often stronger if it is in writing. A colleague of mine asks his patients to carry a small book with them in which they write their plan and sign a commitment to carry it out. Each week he and the patient review what the patient did to fulfill his commitment. The patient writes their evaluation in the book. The therapist finds written commitments help his patients gain the discipline to fulfill their plans. As lawyers have always known, it is harder to escape from a written agreement than from a verbal one. Furthermore, the notebook carries my colleague into the person's life; their involvement continues during the week because of what the patient has written in his book during the therapy hour. It also avoids argument about the content of the plan and about whether or not the commitment to the plan was fulfilled. A therapist or other helper, however, cannot expect a commitment, written or verbal, to be fulfilled until there is involvement, until the person's current behavior has been examined and evaluated, and until a good plan has been made.

6. ACCEPT NO EXCUSES. When a person does not fulfill his commitment, a common occurrence, the value judgment that preceded the plan must be rechecked. If the value judgment is still valid, then the plan must be reevaluated. If the plan is

reasonable, the person must either recommit himself or state, "I am no longer going to commit myself to this plan." If he says, "I'll no longer commit myself to it," then he is no longer responsible. If he remains committed to the plan, however, the therapist must continue to ask him to honor the commitment. The therapist cannot hold the patient to the commitment in a legal or punitive sense, nor, because of his implicit commitment never to do so, can he withdraw. The only course of action—and it is a powerful one—open to the therapist or helping person is never to excuse the person who needs help from the responsibility of the commitment.

Because no excuses are accepted in Reality Therapy, we rarely ask, "Why?" Hard as it is to refrain, we do not ask, "Why did you do it?" because we believe everyone involved knows the answer. An excuse is the easy way off the hook. We cannot help anyone if we admit that there are valid excuses for not fulfilling a reasonable plan. Valid or not, to become successful, he must fulfill the plan. An excuse reduces the pain of failure, but it does not lead to success. Suppose a man was in danger of losing his job because he was drinking. He stopped drinking and went to work regularly but was laid off anyway because the company lost a major contract. Unable to find another job, he starts drinking again to ease the pain, but his drinking makes it almost impossible to get a new job. The therapist must not accept this reasonable hard-luck story. Instead, a new plan must be made. If the therapist accepts his excuses, the man may never be able to handle future situations of stress.

When someone does not fulfill his commitment, we do not emphasize his failure. We do not say, "It's your fault, you failed, you've done wrong." We simply ask, "Are you still going to try to fulfill the commitment? If you say you are, then when?" We wait; time is rarely a serious obstacle. If we keep our involvement, if we keep making plans and getting commitments, eventually the patient will begin to fulfill them. If the patient tries to make excuses, the therapist should say, "Please, you don't have to make excuses for me." To a patient who arrives late and wants to tell me why or apologize profusely, I say, "You are here. Let's get started." If I have more time, I give it to him. Seeing that the patient is still important to me and the statement, "Let's not talk about it, you are here now, it's your responsibility," seem to solve the problem in most cases.

The therapist must insist that a commitment made is worth keeping. The only commitments many failures have made are to their irresponsibilities, their emotions, and their involvement with themselves. These commitments have mired them deeply in failure. The therapist cannot help unless he and the patient are both willing to reexamine the plan continually and make a mutual decision either to renew the commitment, if the plan is valid, or to give it up, if it is not. The therapist must say to the patient, "If you are not going to do it, say so, but don't say you are and then give excuses when you fail." Excuses are bad in almost all situations, whether between husband and wife, parent and child, or teacher and student. Excuses, rationalizations, and intellectualizations can become the death knell of any successful relationship; they have no place in Reality Therapy.

To do Reality Therapy well requires the ability not to accept excuses, not to probe for fault, not to be a detective to find out Why. Reality Therapy assumes that a commitment, according to a reasonable plan, can always be fulfilled. A good therapist never gives up. His tenacity helps the patient gain the experience of fulfilling a commitment to a responsible plan, possibly for the first time in his life. Many of the girls at the Ventura School for Delinquent Girls told me, "Dr. Glasser, I knew you cared about me when you didn't take the excuse." Excuses let people off the hook; they provide temporary relief, but they eventually lead to more failure and a failure identity. Any time we take an excuse when we are trying to help a person gain a successful identity, we do him harm.

7. NO PUNISHMENT. Not to punish is as important as not to take excuses. Eliminating punishment is very difficult for most people who are successful to accept because they believe that part of their success stems from their fear that punishment will follow failure. We believe punishment breaks the involvement necessary for the patient to succeed. When he does succeed, we give praise. Unlike punishment, praise solidifies the involvement. Punishment is any treatment of another person that causes him pain, physical or mental. Praise, always involving, leads to more responsible behavior. The purpose of punishment is to change someone's behavior through fear, pain, or loneliness. If it were an effective means of getting people to change, we would have few failures in our society. Many incompetent and irresponsible people have been punished over and over again throughout their lives with little beneficial effect. Instead punishment reinforces their loneliness. Confirming their belief that no one cares about them, it drives them further into self-involvement and increases their hostility or their isolation or both.

For many delinquents punishment serves as a source of involvement. They receive attention through delinquent behavior, if only that of the police, court, probation counselor, and prison. The punishment is painful, but it is better than being alone. In addition, it somewhat reduces the pain of failure. A failing person rationalizes the punishment as a reason for the anger that caused him to be hostile. He considers his behavior to be revenge against those who punish him. Punishment, if immediate and severe, may deter the individual from doing the same thing again. If we immediately slap a child's hand when he touches something he should not, he may learn "Hands off!" He may also learn to be more crafty; punishment may motivate him to be a more careful criminal.

Mild punishment is sometimes effective when it serves to remind people that better options are open than their present choice. If no other options are open, punishment is of no use. The severe punishment of pre-Victorian England did little to deter crime because the people had few options and little hope for survival anyway. Many committed crimes as a means of legal suicide. People who are successful and who have various options available may be deterred by punishment. Nowhere is this shown more clearly than in the men who pleaded guilty to Watergate crimes. If there were no punishment or threat of punishment, it is likely they would not have admitted their guilt. Moderate punishment, however, will probably not only reform them for life but it will also have a strong deterrent effect in the future upon others like them who will think seriously before they break the law. Thus, if punishment has any value, it is for successful people, but they usually do not need punishment or the example of it to continue behaving successfully. When we punish a child, we take a chance of breaking the involvement. We make a value judgment when we say, "You did wrong and we're going to punish you for it." When we punish, we do not allow the child to evaluate his own behavior. The often-punished child gains no experience in making judgments; later, as an adult, he often judges erratically and poorly because he has had no preparation for being on his own, and he repeats this pattern with his children. It is important that therapists, parents, and teachers do not punish directly with beatings and threats or indirectly with ridicule or withdrawal.

Reasonably agreed-upon consequences of irresponsible behavior are not punishment. A parent who makes a plan with his son to allow him certain privileges if he accepts certain responsibilities is no longer bound to the plan if his son fails in his accepted responsibilities. If the parent says, "You can use the family car on Saturday nights providing you wash it once a week," and the son does not wash the car, then the parent can, and should, refuse the son use of the car. The parent is holding to the agreement. The son will learn nothing if the parent does not have the discipline to fulfill his part of the plan. The son needs only to wash the car to be able to use it. It would, however, be excessive and punitive for the parent to say, "Since you failed to wash the car, you can't use it for six Saturday nights." Even if the son, under pressure, had agreed to this condition, it would be a bad plan because it would invite resentment over a major loss for a mild transgression. Certainly, if he did not wash the car that week, he should be deprived of it for that Saturday night, but as soon as he washes it, he fulfills his part of the bargain and can have the car again. This arrangement is not punitive; it is a reasonable and acceptable plan. The son may be upset over losing the car if he fails to wash it, but he can understand why his parent stands firm and he knows his parent still cares about him.

The parent who lets the son use the car anytime while casually asking him to keep it clean, and then suddenly says, "Well, you don't wash it enough, so you can't have it anymore for a while," is punitive and irrational. The son, with no preparation for this capricious behavior by the parent, reacts by being less involved, by loving, respecting, and listening to the parent less. He must look to others for models of successful behavior. If no other models are available, the child has a good chance, because of the capricious, punitive behavior of the parent, of beginning to identify himself as a failure and of acting in failing ways.

The examples in the following chapters show that problems can be solved without punishment. Punishment was devised by people with power, and power thrives on punishment, threat, and isolation. In a survival society, powerful people use punishment to keep control. In the identity society, however, internal control is needed instead of external control. Successful people believe punishment will change behavior because they fear failure themselves, but failures do not fear failure, they identify with it.

Because punishment reduces involvement and causes failures to identify more securely with their failure, we must learn not to use it. We must eliminate punishment as a major weapon of government and institutions, families and marriages, social organizations and individual relationships. Giving praise for a job well done instead of rejection for a job below expectations will motivate people toward success.

Chapter Five

The Family in the
Identity Society

Because more families are breaking up than ever before, the family may seem more dispensable than it was in the past. The contrary is probably true. Until another institution can provide a role for children—and none, including the kibbutz, is in sight—the family continues to be indispensable. Although other institutions, such as the schools, may augment the family, none can effectively replace its function. Because divorce is common, many children in our society have no intact family to help them toward a successful role. These children, with less family involvement, often have a difficult task gaining a successful identity. Many fail and, hostile about their failure, place a heavy burden on society.

Steve and Beth Sutton are satisfactorily married; they care for each other, intend to stay married, and have decided to raise children. Steve and Beth do not need children to help them survive. They want to raise a family to help them each extend and maintain their identities by taking on the new roles of father and mother. Expecting that the involvement potential of the family will serve as role reinforcement for all of them, they want to build a family that can function successfully within the identity society. At the planning stage, Steve and Beth recognize, albeit somewhat dimly, that it takes work to rear and stay involved with a child when he is an economic liability. In the past, when children were assets, involvement, goal-oriented though it may have been, was mandatory. Now it is not.

Children, like everyone else, need love, support, and warm, human involvement. Steve and Beth will discover that in the beginning giving love is the easiest part of raising a child. It is easy to love a small child and get him to respond to your love. It is harder to continue to give him love, involvement, and guidance toward goals as he grows older. Involvement in a large family, including grandparents and other relatives, was a normal part of survival societies. In the identity society involvement must be gained in the presence of fewer people. Steve and Beth, living away from their parents, brothers, and sisters, must help Mike, their first child, become comfortable with both friends and strangers and learn the skill of talking and listening to them.

Beth and Steve realize that Mike must have a great deal of involvement; thus as their family is small, he needs nonfamily socialization. In addition to involvement with people outside the family, there should be plenty of family fun and rough-housing with this little guy who is not a hothouse plant but a strong child. Beth sees that Mike is exposed to normal noisy household activity and that people do not tread softly around him. She exposes him to other babies who may share his playpen for short periods and to older children and adults who hold and talk to him, and she takes him out in all weather. She lets him be held by young people and old people as well as other parents to show him that people are warm, friendly, and safe. New surroundings should be a part of Mike's early life. Exposing him to new people in new surroundings with Beth or Steve near to give him the security he needs will help him make the transition from his parents to strangers. In addition to many people and various surroundings, he needs time alone in his crib and playpen to learn to create activities by himself. Mike needs a balance—time with others and time by himself.

Steve and Beth will do Mike a favor if they do not worry about his health. The Suttons need to develop confidence that Mike is sturdy; he does not need continual medical supervision to stay healthy. Parents can be assured that their baby is healthy if he is happy, sleeps well, eats well, and is comfortable in social situations. A child who does not sleep, eat, and play well may also be healthy, but he is certainly healthy if he does. Because involvement is so important, socialization rather than health, which is rarely a concern, should be stressed. Many parents have their priorities mixed, and as a result there are many physically healthy failures in our society. Early socialization, teaching a child to be comfortable with and enjoy the company of various people, is the best experience parents can provide. It puts the child on the road to a successful life in the identity society.

Early socialization must be expanded from passive to active between ages two and five. The age of transition depends on the maturity and intelligence of the child and the time the Suttons have available. As soon as Mike is able to talk, he should be listened to. Mike should talk with as many people as possible. He needs a chance to talk with his friends, parents, and as many people as are normally a part of his life. In the past, the large family, with grandparents, uncles, aunts, and cousins around, probably handled the transition to active socialization on the part of the child more adequately than today's family does. Now, small mobile families must make a conscious effort to see that their children become involved with family and friends.

I consider television a danger to children between ages two and five because they should then be learning, by playing with each other, to socialize and communicate. Children need many social experiences to gain confidence in their ability to be involved. The greatest obstacle to a child's socialization, an obstacle probably as harmful to success in the identity society as being malnourished was dangerous to life in the survival society, is excessive viewing of television. Few parents realize how much their preschool child watches television. I was surprised myself to read a report of Dr. Gerald L. Looney, of the University of Arizona, to the American Academy of Pediatrics, citing research that a prekindergarten child spends 64 percent of his waking time before a television set. Few children staring at television this much will learn the necessary social skills with their peers or with adults at an age when they are best able to do so. I suggest that the time a child watches television be restricted during this formative age to short periods. Restricting television time is difficult for many parents because the television set serves as a mechanical companion that holds the child's interest, asks nothing of him, and frees the parent for other chores.

Daily in most homes one or several children sit in front of the television set. Television is a passive, nonsocial medium that stimulates a child's nervous system enough to make him feel comfortable but does not fulfill his nervous system's need for involvement because it deprives him of social play with others. It is analogous to feeding a child only candy, cake, and ice cream. Although he will feel comfortable and even enjoy this diet for a while, it will damage his health. Watching television by himself, or even in the company of others, is almost totally nonsocial. It falsely fulfills the child's needs for involvement and temporarily satisfies him, but he does not learn to get along with others. In school, when he is not and cannot be confronted in this passive yet stimulating way, he reacts with apathy, confusion, or antagonism because he has not learned the social skills he needs to get along with others.

Because I work extensively in elementary schools, I am often asked to suggest ways to cope with five- to ten-year-old children who seem to have no social responsibility. They cannot cooperate in the necessary give and take of the classroom. Often disrupting the class because they cannot settle down or listen, they sometimes overwhelm the teacher with their senseless, erratic activity. When asked to become actively involved in learning (to read, for example), they are passive. Used to receiving, they do not know how to put forth an effort. I believe there is a cause-and-effect relationship between excess viewing of television at a young age and this recent hyperactivity syndrome in children in elementary school. If I am right, parents should limit the time their young children watch TV. Reasonable limits might be thirty minutes a day at age two, and an hour to an hour and a half a day at ages three to six. Limiting television, however, is not the entire answer. A child must play with other children to learn social skills in an active, normal setting.

A currently popular explanation for the hyperactivity seen in children is that they have a brain abnormality that has suddenly become almost epidemic. No reason is given for this abnormality in which the brain seems to stimulate the child with bursts of erratic, nervous energy that cause the hyperactivity. Once this diagnosis is made, drugs (amphetamines) are prescribed to calm the abnormal brain activity and make the child less active. I believe that this new epidemic may be caused by the frustration of the neural need for involvement left unsatisfied when the child watches too much television. In that case we should depend less on drugs and more on socially and intellectually stimulating schools. Evidence from our work in the schools suggests that when we make the schools better, such problems are greatly reduced. Although drugs may calm the child enough to allow the learning of social involvement to begin, they need be little used if television watching is limited and the home and school provide active involvement.

Steve and Beth want to give Mike time with other children, but they have found that there are not as many children in the immediate neighborhood as there were when Steve and Beth were young. To give Mike opportunities for social play, Steve and Beth should enroll him in a nursery school, a Head Start program, or a program arranged with other parents in their neighborhood. Beth may ask advice from local nursery schools if she and other mothers want to arrange a program.

Whenever possible, Mike should be on his own; Beth should let him learn to handle himself with his friends. She should stay in the background, stepping in only when he is doing something dangerous or when he is socially over his head. There may be a little rough-and-tumble—good for little girls as well as little boys—arguing, and fighting, with crying and tantrums as a natural consequence of the hurt feelings. Because Mike must learn to handle social discord, he should not be protected from the social facts of life among his friends. Mike learns to communicate by discovering the skills he needs to make his wants and feelings known. Learning his value and his limits relative to others his age, he is not socially out of his depth or overwhelmed when he is competing against and playing with other children between ages two and five. He cannot get too much good play.

Mike himself can usually judge when to stop playing. If he becomes tired and cranky, or if he is obviously beyond his capacity to handle a situation, Steve or Beth should step in to give him a chance to rest, either by himself or with them in a quiet, warm situation. At such times, Beth learns not to take the easy way of setting him in front of a television set that gives passive, nonhuman respite. It is better at these times that he play by himself with his own toys, learn to appreciate his own company, and develop his own fantasies without the assistance of television's commercial fantasies. If he can learn to be at ease with himself, enjoy his toys, amuse himself with books, and interest himself by exploring his environment, he learns that being alone can be pleasant and rewarding, rather than painful. To be lonely is always bad, but the ability to be alone without being upset is vital.

Learning to talk and listen to adults is also important for children between ages two and five. Later, social and often vocational success depends on a person's skill to present himself well and hold his own in conversation. A young child can participate in thoughtful discussions with his family. (How such discussions can occur in school is described in *Schools Without Failure*, Chapters 10 to 12.) A child should be stimulated by his parents' questions, and they should listen to his responses. For example, when Mike is three, Steve or Beth might casually ask him why he likes to eat certain foods. "Why do you like ice cream?" might be a starter. Discuss his ideas with him in a nonjudgmental way that allows him to think about his preferences for various foods. Ask him if he likes all kinds of ice cream or if he would like ice cream instead of other things to eat. Although Steve and Beth should get him to make a few value judgments, they must be easy and nonjudgmental when he says something they do not agree with. When Mike is five, Beth might ask him why he wants to go to Disneyland or, after a visit, what he liked and did not like. She might ask him about any ideas he has to improve Disneyland. Beth wants to get him to think, and she listens to what he says. Intellectual discussions in which Mike has to think and respond prepare him for the world he lives in; they help him learn to discriminate, question, and express himself.

Steve and Beth must not "down" Mike or make him feel inadequate. Thinking of good questions that stimulate thoughtful replies and listening to what he says with an accepting attitude, they never say or imply, "I know all, I'm an adult, you know nothing. We are just playing a game to see how much more I know than you." If, when Mike is between the critical ages of two and five, the Suttons talk to him in an involving and nonjudgmental way, if they compliment him when he does good thinking, if they listen carefully to what he says, and if they get him to formulate and express his thoughts clearly, they will teach him to communicate with both children and adults.

Whenever possible Steve and Beth should say yes to the requests and demands that Mike makes as he grows up. Too many parents raise their children with a no, rather than a yes, attitude. To any nonroutine request, they say no; after the child nags and complains, they often reconsider and say yes. This is bad because it teaches their child that wheedling and tantrums have more to do with favorable decisions than merit. It closes honest give and take and opens up cleverness and tantrums, rather than reason, as a means of child-parent problem solving. Parents who say yes as much as possible raise children who respect a no when it is needed. Seeing that his parents are reasonable, a child learns to respect their judgment.

For instance, if Mike at age twelve to fourteen asks to go somewhere Beth has never been and knows little about, she should not immediately say no and later be wheedled into saying yes. She should say, "Yes, you can go if you discuss the situation with me and satisfy my doubts." They should discuss safety problems, Mike's companions, and costs. If he can make a reasonable case, she will let him go. If Mike has been raised in a "yes" atmosphere, he can accept a refusal when concerns of his parents are not met reasonably. The attitude "yes, until no is proved," rather than "no, until yes is proved," is important for good communication between parent and child. If there is good involvement, Mike will understand his parents' concern and will not continually make demands that must be refused.

School presents problems to Mike and his parents. In the identity society, a child's schooling is such an important pathway to status and success (for the parents as well as for the child) that Steve and Beth will certainly be concerned about Mike's education. Most parents who have completed high school or college become concerned about a child's college prospects when he is very young. I hear children in elementary school discuss their grade point averages. In the East, concern over college entrance has been carried to absurd extremes; some nursery schools advertise the percentage of their "graduates" who enter Ivy League colleges, thus implying that the experience in their nursery school will be a help toward this goal. The select nursery school helps a child more by alleviating his parents' anxiety—and thus reducing the pressure on him—than through any tangible program the school may offer.

In *Schools Without Failure*, I discussed the school's need to foster involvement with children, to educate them in relevant ways, and to insist upon a thinking curriculum that does not emphasize memorization, right answers, and grades. Because goal-oriented schools often fail role-oriented students, Beth and Steve must ensure through role-oriented upbringing at home that Mike has an identity strong enough to counterbalance the goal-oriented school he will attend. They must help Mike through the goal-oriented school system by making him feel successful in school. One way Steve and Beth can help Mike is not to demand too much of him in his first few school years. They will not expect Mike to be a genius, compare him with other children, or worry if he is not excelling in everything. If Mike does not read by Christmas in the first grade or if he does not later quickly learn to spell or do arithmetic, Steve and Beth should be accepting. They should understand that some children advance more slowly than others. Also, Mike may perceive how silly much of school is and refuse to learn in the beginning.

Because the skills—reading well, writing clearly, speaking effectively, and doing arithmetic accurately—are most important in elementary school, Steve and Beth need not be concerned if Mike does not learn the facts courses readily. They should read to or with him and help him with his school work for involvement as well as for tutoring. If he is to gain self-worth, however, they must not do too much of his homework. To help Mike both to learn and to express himself, they can discuss with him television, articles in newspapers, movies that he attends, sporting events, and even material possessions such as cars or bikes. If Mike can read satisfactorily by grade six and has some intellectual curiosity, he is all right. The knowledge courses and even the math are less important.

Schools would be more effective if time were allotted for games that require thinking. Steve and Beth should play games such as chess, checkers, Monopoly, and cards with Mike. Children can learn much from these games; it is too bad they are frowned on in many schools. A good parent will let his child win some games at first. The child needs time to learn and enough victories to keep him from quitting before he learns. Once the child gains skill, the parent can play as hard as he wants; his child will be a match. An excellent game I play with my children is cribbage. The children think, make choices, and learn a little about probability. Because the game is short and not intensively concentrated, it forms a good background for talk between child and parent. Children learn and have fun through games. The more fun Mike can have with his parents, the more secure he will be in his role and the more he will learn in school.

Steve and Beth should be relaxed about report cards. Each time the elementary school teacher gives grades, she must make about thirty evaluations per child. Teachers have no basis for making so many discrete evaluations with any degree of accuracy. Steve or Beth should go over Mike's report card with him, emphasize his strengths, and say to him, "Let's work on a few of the weaknesses." Then they or someone else can help him. They should neither punish Mike for low grades nor reward him materially for good grades. Despite the destructive effect of report cards on many children, elementary schools continue to give them. But if the parents continue to support the child, they need not fear that he will be a school failure because of a bad elementary school report card. Steve and Beth should request a conference with

Mike's teacher if his report card is not as good as they believe it should be, and they should support the teacher when she discusses her plans to help Mike during this conference. Mike should be there so that both he and his teacher learn that Steve and Beth are parents who care about what Mike does in school.

Because reading is basic to success in school, families are tense in which children do not read or read poorly. If Mike reads poorly, Steve and Beth should buy some easy, interesting reading material, such as comic books, classic comics, and books with illustrations, to read to him and for him to read himself. They can encourage Mike to read the funnies or any other part of the newspaper that interests him, such as the sports page. As Mike grows older, Steve and Beth will not become nervous if he reads magazines such as *Playboy* with a little antiseptic sex. Reading is reading; it is best to encourage him to read whatever piques his interest.

It is important that the Suttons refrain from comparing Mike with his brothers, sisters, cousins, or themselves, if either Mike or anyone else is hurt by the comparison. Parents must never compare a child directly with an older brother or sister by saying, "When he was this age, he did so and so," thereby placing the child in a position where he cannot compete. Fair competition is valuable because it can be involving and fun. Competition in school is often unfair because the same children always win, making it uninvolving and dull for the others. Children in the classroom who are highly competent in similar skills probably are stimulated by competition. Because the skills of children are variable, competition must take the differences into account to be fair. Steve can mention anything Mike is doing better than he did or better than a relative did at a similar age. A motivating and fun comparison that will help Mike feel successful can usually be found. As Mike continues through school, his parents should help him plan his program. Although Mike must take certain courses if he wishes to go to college, Steve and Beth should not urge him to take difficult technical courses that he may not be interested in. They should help him plan a balanced program that includes the arts, humanities, and applied arts. High school counselors, often under parental pressure to get boys like Mike into college, rarely balance the program of a good student. Steve and Beth can help Mike investigate entrance requirements for a few colleges of his choice; they should not depend entirely on the overworked school counselor for this information. Mike can best choose his high school program and get the most help from his counselor if he knows specific college requirements. Also, academic planning in high school is good practice for similar planning in college.

Any subject is valuable that involves Mike, that does not place undue importance on grades, and that he sees as relevant to his life. The academic subjects are made less and less relevant because of the noninvolved lecture method of teaching them and by emphasis on grades, competition, and memorization of trivia. Teachers ask obscure questions to rank and grade children on a scale or "normal curve."* The students are trapped because many of these subjects are required for college. Almost every child in America takes tenth-grade geometry, yet even students going into science could be taught all they need to know about geometry in two or three weeks. Nevertheless, Mike and his friends are dragged through years of such subjects as an exercise in attrition and endurance, for the child, the teacher, and the parent who tries to help the child.

* See *Schools Without Failure*, pp. 70–72.

Steve and Beth should take Mike to plays, concerts, and movies to widen his intellectual horizons. They may ask him to watch with them television programs selected for artistic or intellectual content. Discussions that follow these events help build involvement and challenge Mike to think. Steve and Beth should encourage Mike to take courses in music, drama, art, and debate at school. As interested members of the community, Steve and Beth should support efforts to keep these subjects in the school curriculum, rather than idly watch them be cut as frills by those who still adhere solely to the "three R's."

Mike's social life is an important part of his development as a person. Even before he reaches school age, and certainly from then on, Steve and Beth should welcome Mike's friends to their home. Little extra planning is necessary to have enough food in the house to invite a friend to enjoy dinner with the family. Welcoming his friends will help both parents and children bridge the new cultural gap. The effort necessary to feed extra children or having some additional noise at dinner is worthwhile because it helps Mike feel that people are welcome and important at his house. As an added bonus the Suttons will find that when they associate with Mike's friends in a warm, friendly manner, these young people are most delightful and, in many cases, more fun than adults. However, they will not be delightful unless Steve and Beth make them genuinely and completely welcome in their home. If they do so, Mike's friends will respect the rules of his home even when Steve and Beth are not there.

As children grow they like some status in the home. For example, each child can have a chance to sit at the head of the table if everyone changes his seat occasionally. If Steve always has the best seat, Mike feels slighted; Papa Bear's chair should be shared by the children as they grow. Sharing the front seat of the car with Dad seems very important to a young child, and driving the family gives confidence and support to an older child with a license.

Reading at the table is not bad, especially at breakfast when people are usually not talkative anyway. At dinner parents and children should talk to each other rather than read, listen to the radio, or watch television. If Mike understands that Steve and Beth will listen to his thoughts at this time, he will look forward to dinner and conversation with his parents.

The above suggestions help a child begin to discover a role. Goals should not be neglected, and one important goal, family finances, should be discussed clearly with children from the time they are old enough to understand money. Mike should understand the money the family has, where it comes from, and how it can and cannot be spent. The money is not Steve's money, Beth's money, or Mike's money; rather it belongs to the family. Although the parents decide how most of it is spent, the children should share in the decisions, especially when the decisions concern them. As soon as Mike can understand, Steve and Beth should talk to him about major family purchases, such as homes, home improvements, furniture, cars, motorcycles, and vacations. Contrary to popular belief, Steve and Beth will often find that Mike, rather than being profligate with the family money, will probably be a more conservative spender than they are when he is allowed to share in purchasing decisions. He will learn practical economics relevant to family education. Parents should also teach teen-age children about checking accounts, charge accounts, loans, bank interest, mortgages, and insurance. Knowledge of family finance will help them operate financially for the rest of their lives.

The Suttons may or may not give Mike an allowance. Personally I am not enthusiastic about allowances because they put undue emphasis on money. Sometimes Mike may feel desperate because his allowance is not enough for something he wants; at other times he may worry that he must spend it all to keep Steve and Beth from reducing the allowance. If the use of an allowance is discussed and understood, however, it can be an excellent way to teach children to handle money. Parents can teach children about money whether or not they give them an allowance by discussing the children's wants with them nonjudgmentally, and then giving the children the money to buy what they have agreed on. The Suttons should not imply to Mike that they have money when they do not, nor should they pretend that they do not when they do.

Drinking and smoking are of vital concern to many parents. If you do not want your child to smoke, you should not smoke yourself. The parent who smokes heavily has little credibility when he tells his child not to smoke. The same reasoning applies to drinking. Steve and Beth should discuss smoking and drinking with Mike so he knows what they think. Mike should not be lectured on the evils of something that the Suttons show, by their actions, they do not consider evil. If parents think drinking is wrong, they have the right to lecture their child on the subject providing they do not drink themselves. If parents drink in moderation, a child will learn to handle alcohol better by seeing them practice moderation than by listening to lectures or discussions. Steve and Beth should understand that if they lecture against a practice that many people, including Mike's peers, accept, they may lose their credibility. A parent cannot usually expect to influence a child's attitude so much that the child remains aloof to the attitude of the world. Steering the middle course by comparing the world's attitude with their attitude, Steve and

Beth should try to help Mike make a reasonable decision himself.

The Suttons should not expect Mike to make the same decisions about school, work, girls, alcohol, and cars that they made. Reared in an identity society, Mike has different insecurities and fears from those Steve and Beth had. Mike can make some decisions more easily and with less fear than they could at his age, but with others he may have more trouble—sometimes because he has more options. The Suttons must act as a sounding board, perhaps a devil's advocate, to help Mike make important decisions such as his career. Once he makes a decision, they should urge him to make a plan and commit himself to it wholeheartedly for a reasonable time. The Suttons should discuss any consequences arising from Mike's decision so he learns that good planning is a continuing process. As Mike grows older, Steve and Beth should ask him to become involved in their plans; if they do so, he will often ask his parents to become involved in his plans. For example, if Steve lets Mike help him select a car, he will find, when Mike looks for a car, that Mike wants Steve to help him. Steve's experience helps Mike make a better selection than he might make on his own.

As Mike grows older, his choice of friends becomes another concern for Steve and Beth. Many people think children should have friends like themselves, an attitude based on the idea that one is safer if he sticks to his own. Having friends like oneself may be easier and provide fewer problems than choosing friends of various backgrounds, but it also limits one's involvement and learning. The Suttons should develop an openness toward Mike's friends. If he brings home a friend with shoulder-length hair, with shabby clothes, or of a different race, the Suttons should accept him. If Mike has a success identity, he will usually choose friends who also have success identities; if occasionally he does not, his parents need not be concerned. Once invited into the house, any friend who becomes involved with Mike and his family will rarely influence Mike toward bad goals and decisions. Refusing to allow a friend to visit shows a lack of confidence in Mike. Lack of confidence weakens the family involvement and may cause Mike's involvement with his friend to become stronger. The friend's ideas might conflict with those of the Suttons, but Mike may be more influenced by a friend who is rejected by his family than he would be if the friend were welcome. Although many parents now accept most of what their children do, children should not expect their parents to accept behavior, such as drug use, that they know their parents strongly oppose.

In high school and college Mike will probably be exposed to students from a wider background than his parents were at his age. Schools are bigger, and they draw from larger, more varied populations. Rarely concerned about survival, young people usually accept other people readily; they are confident that they can associate with diverse people because their survival is not threatened. They test their parents to see if they are willing to tolerate and, more, to welcome people of diverse backgrounds and interests. The more Steve and Beth accept Mike's friends, the more they will help Mike look rationally at many kinds of people. Smoke screens of lies or intolerance that conflict with what they profess to stand for will cause Mike to distrust his parents and reduce his involvement with them. The Suttons' acceptance of Mike's friends is extremely important to maintain and increase family involvement.

Another matter of deep concern to Steve and Beth is how

Mike and his little sister Anne behave sexually as they begin to mature. There is no particularly appropriate time, place, or situation to tell Mike or Anne about the facts of life; it should be a natural part of family growth and may be discussed in terms of new children being born into the family or neighboring families. Mike and Anne are early exposed to sexual stimuli as they watch television, read magazines, or listen to their friends. They probably become acutely conscious of sex around the fifth grade. Some children engage in kissing and petting from elementary school on. The Suttons are concerned because they know petting may lead to sexual intercourse, and they do not want Mike or Anne to mistake sexual involvement for the deeper personal involvement necessary for a mature sexual relationship. Becoming sexually involved may mean a pregnancy for Anne or a forced early marriage for either. Knowing that a long education is necessary for most good jobs in the identity society, they fear that if Mike or Anne becomes sexually involved, he or she will not finish college. They discuss with friends whether mothers should give their daughters the Pill.

When Mike and Anne start serious dating, Steve and Beth should explain to them the responsibilities involved with sex. Children who begin a sexual relationship will often come to a parent when problems arise if communication is open. Anne may be pregnant, Mike may have caused a pregnancy, or either may think he has a venereal disease. If Anne is engaged in a sexual relationship with a boyfriend, she may talk to Beth about it and, if necessary, have Beth help her obtain adequate contraceptive protection. Beth should discuss with Anne the hazards of a sexual relationship without commitment, if this is indeed the case. As Anne and Mike grow up, Steve and Beth should try to show them what commitment is.

The best way Steve and Beth can help Mike and Anne is for each to show his commitment to the other. In the context of commitment, Mike and Anne should help with some of the duties and responsibilities of the home. As they share family and home duties, they learn that hard work and commitment bind a family together and help make it successful. They will then have a good idea of the duties and responsibilities toward the opposite sex.

Most parents easily welcome young friends into the house, but they have some hesitancy as the friends become older and may indulge in kissing, petting, and drinking. Steve and Beth should make Mike's teen-age and college friends welcome. Making sure everyone is comfortable, they should get to know them, joke with them, and tell them a *little* about how they dated at that age. When children do not feel that their friends are welcome in their home, they often meet just as couples in cars. Without parental involvement and under biological stress, young people may engage in sexual activity before they are involved. If sexual relations occur without involvement, the girl almost always and the boy usually will feel failure.

When the Suttons have friends visiting, the children should be included in the adult group for a while. Children involved with their parents and interested in other people want to meet their parents' friends because the friends are important to their parents. Although children need not stay for the whole evening or sit at the table at a formal dinner, before dinner children can be introduced and given a chance to talk with their parents' friends. Steve and Beth invite people to their home because they believe them to be interesting and worthwhile; by meeting and talking to these people, their children learn to understand adults. Because involvement with successful people is the key to a successful identity, parents must ensure for their children as much and as varied experience with people as they can.

Steve and Beth should encourage their children to pursue individual interests in or out of school, and they should buy them what they need to pursue these interests. They should not immediately buy expensive stamp albums, coin collections, tools, or electronic kits, but they should provide necessary funds to allow Mike to start. They can tell him that as he expands his interest and convinces them that he receives value from his pursuit, they will give him more money if he wants more equipment. If the family finances are an open book, Mike knows what the family can afford. If he loses interest after a while, the Suttons should not feel the money has been poorly spent. Because interests change often in the identity society, the Suttons must understand that Mike probably will not be involved in just one interest as he might have been in the survival society in which changing an interest was more difficult than it is now.

Today we live in a society in which travel, even world travel, once the exclusive privilege of the rich, is common. Steve and Beth contemplate trips to places their parents barely read about, much less considered traveling to. When the children are young, the Suttons will take trips as a family, and these trips can be good or bad. Many people mistakenly attempt extensive vacations with young children. With only a limited ability to appreciate new surroundings, children do not enjoy extensive and complicated sightseeing. They cannot have acquired the background necessary to enjoy long visits to museums that fascinate adults. They like nature, especially if they can meet nature actively by walking through redwood forests or swimming in mountain streams. Spending money on an expensive trip of little interest to Mike and Anne, and then insisting that they appreciate the marvelous opportunity, needlessly strains the family involvement. Basic to all Steve's and Beth's relationships to their children should be the understanding that the children may not necessarily value or be ready for what Steve and Beth believe to be important. When the children are very young, it is usually desirable for the Suttons to find someone to care for them at home while the parents take a vacation by themselves. A baby-sitter is often cheaper than taking the children along and serves to cultivate trust in Mike and Anne for others.

During the middle years, when Mike and Anne are nine through eighteen, the family can take vacations that give the children an opportunity to pursue their interests. If the Suttons are sensitive to what their children enjoy, these vacations can be wonderful family experiences. Steve and Beth should prepare Mike and Anne before the family leaves so they understand something about the places they are going. As the children get older, they can help plan vacations as well as other family activities. Steve and Beth should consider taking a friend along for Mike and Anne. Many parents will pay their child's share of a vacation with another family, and when children have their friends along, the vacation is usually better for all.

The Suttons should make clear certain rules that are necessary for everyone to enjoy the vacation. Children who know reasonable bounds will tolerate some discomfort on a vacation without too much complaining. If the children argue and fight, the vacation should not be an annual event. After vacationing by themselves for one year, the parents can discuss with the children where the family might go together the following year if the rules are observed. Parents with a rarely used Ping-Pong table at home find their children play at a vacation hotel for hours at a time because they are meeting new and interesting children. The Suttons should not lecture Mike and Anne by saying, "Why don't you use our Ping-Pong table? You're using the one here so much." The situation is different, and Steve and Beth should not expect their children to respond as they do at home. If Anne and Mike can find new friends on their own, they will not continually pester their parents for attention. When the children make friends, they may introduce Steve and Beth to their parents, making the Suttons' adult part of the vacation more enjoyable.

As Mike and Anne grow older, they may want to go away to camp. Various kinds of camps should be investigated as possibilities. For families of limited means, parents can sometimes find YMCA camps, charity-sponsored camps, or community-fund-sponsored camps that are often excellent. Parents need initiative to make sure that their child has a chance to go to these camps. Some children gain from camping; others do not. A good camping experience depends on the counselors' ability to involve the children with one another in meaningful games and activities.

Besides camping and traveling with the family, Mike and Anne may want to travel without their parents. Teen tours offer supervised travel. Steve and Beth with Mike or Anne should talk to young people who have taken these tours and to their parents. Parents should ask for references and investigate thoroughly before allowing their child to take such tours. The investigation can provide good involvement and an opportunity for Mike and Anne to develop judgment. If the tour will not give references, it is a good idea to skip it.

By age sixteen, Mike or Anne may want to travel alone

or with a few friends without adult supervision. At this time there is often a serious conflict between parent and child. If Mike or Anne wants to go alone, I believe the Suttons have good cause for worry and should attempt to stop the child by saying no and providing no support. If they want to go with friends, there should be places on the trip where they can contact adults whom the Suttons already know or whom they can get to know before the trip. The Suttons are concerned that Anne will be criminally attacked, seduced, or robbed, but these hazards are far less likely to occur than most people fear. If both parents and children investigate the trip carefully, and if Anne and Mike honestly tell their parents where they are going and what they plan to do, there is usually little danger. Parents must attempt to judge whether the child will go even if they say no. If the parents believe the child will go without their permission, it is usually better to give permission because the child may then at least listen to the parents' concerns. Parents should not be upset if the child seems to scoff at their worries; he is displaying bravado in the safety of home. When he is on his way, much of what the parents say will be heeded. Children with success identities plan reasonable trips; children with failure identities trek aimlessly around the country by the thousands. If Mike believes in himself, he will avoid trouble on trips better than many adults because he does not have the hangups, the loneliness, the inability to communicate, and the drinking habits that many adults have. If Steve and Beth are careful not to burden Mike with their own inadequacies and if they can appreciate that he is probably more capable than they give him credit for, they will have little cause for worry when he leaves on a trip. Completing a trip successfully—meeting many new people and handling many new experiences—will reinforce his successful identity.

Steve and Beth should expect some work around the house from Mike and Anne. Although regular chores are not so necessary today with our household machinery and supermarket products, I believe some duties, such as washing the car or mowing the lawn, should be a part of every child's growth in a family. Making clear what is expected through family discussion, Steve and Beth should keep the duties reasonably in line with those their children's friends who come from similar homes have. Anne can help with the dishes and some of the housework. Mike can help wash the cars, do some of the gardening and easier repair work, and help his father with household tasks. Except for some of the heavier physical work, the jobs need not be arbitrarily sex-related. Considering the women's liberation movement and the possibility of divorce, each child should have the opportunity to help both parents. Working together provides a good chance for involvement between parents and children. Because a person who works feels worthwhile, some work is good for a very young child. Even a five-year-old can take out the garbage, pick up after father while he is gardening, straighten around the house, or walk the dog. Going to the store, an opportunity not often available in the age of shopping by car, is valuable. Buying something, even food, should be a part of the child's obligation. Although I do not believe children should be paid for help around the house, I do not criticize parents who work out satisfactory pay arrangements.

A child should have some experience in work outside the home. Children need to work; they need to fulfill the obligation of being somewhere on time and to learn to do assigned tasks that they are paid for. Child labor laws make it difficult for children to get jobs. Originally designed to protect children from being exploited, these laws now prevent children from getting jobs that can help them feel worthwhile. Steve and Beth should help Mike and Anne find jobs. They can ask friends, neighbors, customers, or business associates to help find a job for Mike or Anne. When a child works, he should not be asked to spend all of his money for articles his parents ordinarily provide, for then he will have little incentive to work. Decisions about spending money are best worked out in discussions with the child. If the parent is reasonable about how the child spends the money he earns from his first job, the child will probably want to continue to work. Good work is a good way to build a success identity.

A family can do much to help a child feel worthwhile, gain a role within the family, and understand the realities of living within our society. In the next two chapters, I discuss three major problems that may occur while a child is growing up, problems that arise primarily because the conditions described in this chapter are not met.

Chapter Six

Failure in Children:
School Failure

A puzzle today is that so many children who have had so many apparent advantages—economic security, good homes, and doting parents who provide them with many educational and recreational opportunities—are responding to these advantages with failure in school, the use of drugs, and an unwillingness or seeming inability to find and work for reasonable goals. Similar problems are seen in children from homes with little economic security; although there seems to be every reason for them to work hard to get ahead, they seem unable or unwilling to do so. As I have explained in previous chapters, many young people are unable to find an independent role, a satisfactory sense of who they are. Unable to gain love and worth in their relationship with their parents, peers, and teachers, they have identified themselves as failures. A good feeling about oneself—a successful identity—motivates a child toward goals. Children unable to gain a successful identity, whether they come from rich or poor homes, become involved in what I have described in Chapter Three as failure activities.

As a psychiatrist, it seems that almost daily I receive a call or letter from a distraught parent about a child who has "gone bad." Countless articles describe children who fail in school, drop out, use drugs, join the hippie movement, or withdraw in other ways from the goal activities of the identity society; few articles, however, give parents any idea of how to help their children. It is hard for parents to understand why their children fail when they have been raised, in most cases, in homes that have provided many material advantages. Even children from poor homes have had many more advantages than their parents had before them. The children have had love, but too often it has been a giving love with little opportunity for the responsible give-and-take involvement necessary for a child to develop a successful identity.

Distraught because they see their children "going down the drain," husbands accuse wives and wives accuse husbands. They both seek psychiatrists, counselors, ministers, and neighbors for help, asking, "Where have we gone wrong?" Although it is important for them to find out what they did wrong if they have younger children, they must learn what they can do now for the child who seems to them to be in so much trouble. In this chapter, I will try to explain how many parents have erred in their attempts to prepare their children for our new society. More importantly, I will try to explain how parents can help a child in serious trouble to regain a successful identity and begin to work for some of the goals necessary to reinforce and maintain his successful identity.

The most common serious problems of children today are school failure, drug use, and sexual promiscuity. In this chapter, school failure will be discussed; in the next, drug use and sexual promiscuity.

First, let us try to understand why some children from loving, devoted, secure homes are so antagonistic toward their parents and their parents' way of life. Many of the intellectual young blame their parents for being a part of a society that worships materialistic values. They claim they have been raised in an atmosphere in which things are valued more than people. They accuse their parents of being so immersed in keeping up with the Joneses that they have lost touch with their own humanity. How valid these complaints are could be determined only by studying individual cases. In any case, many young people have not been able to become successfully involved with their parents, and they claim that involvement does not occur because their parents value material things over them. Lacking a success identity, many young people turn against their parents first because they know their parents care about them even though they are not involved. After their parents, they turn against society, and, in failing in school, taking drugs, and engaging in promiscuous and un-committed sex, they turn against themselves.

It is a paradox that parents who have taken great pains in raising the children born since 1940, with the hope that they would be the best-adjusted and most motivated generation ever, often have so little to show for their efforts. The main reason that this hope has not been realized is that the parents do not understand the shift in needs from goal to role. Many of them did an excellent job raising their children for a society that no longer exists. About half our children are having difficulties either in finding a successful role or, if they find one, in then finding a goal to work for that supports their role. Unable to find success and handicapped by parents who push them toward goals, the child fails. He fails in school and turns to drugs and sex.

A child with a failure identity, that is, one who lacks a

concept of himself as a loved and worthwhile individual, will not work for any long-term goals. As described in Chapter Three, his life is full of pain, and he lives in a haphazard, erratic struggle to get rid of the pain. Long-term goals seem foreign to a person just trying to feel comfortable today and tomorrow. Even if the child gains a successful independent role, if he does not sometimes between the ages of twelve and twenty achieve some reasonable goals that will support his role, he will slowly lose his successful identity. Many parents have been unable to help their child make this important transition from a successful personal role to working toward goals that further confirm his successful role.

Most parents in our society have gained enough security to become role-oriented, and as they continue to be secure, their role is more and more independent of goal. But the parents have become role-oriented through the traditional sequence described in Chapter One. They still believe that a child should be more concerned with goals that lead to security than with identity. When he is small, his parents' encouragement to enjoy the material advantages of their success helps him gain a successful role. It is a rare preschool child who is not encouraged to have an idependent role. If, however, at six or seven, the secure, loved child does not begin to work for goals—to work hard and to succeed in school, for example—parents begin to worry and urge the child to work hard. Because they do not think that the child can ever succeed in school unless he succeeds from the start, they may punish him. The punishment will weaken or break whatever involvement has been developed.

Because school becomes the measure of the child's ability to succeed in life, if the child does not quickly succeed, the parents fear he is doomed to lifelong failure. Nothing a child does is more important, to most parents, than school. Parents who urge their child to succeed in school are right to encourage him to the extent that the child sees school as important; but many parents push the child so hard that he feels failure and discouragement. The child meets failure because the parent, anxious to see the child get started, begins to reject him if he does not move fast enough. Rejection weakens the child's role because it reduces the involvement between parent and child, setting the stage for failure. A child needs the active involvement and support of his parents longer than most people believe. I think the need remains high until a person is thirty-five to forty years old. Unfortunately, many parents reduce involvement beginning with the child's first failure in school; when the child needs his parents most, he loses them.

A parent who keeps good communication and a warm, open environment does no harm to urge a child to work hard in school. But if the child resists, becoming antagonistic or withdrawn, and if the parent then responds in kind, the child's successful role is often undermined. Rather than work toward a goal that will reinforce his role, the child must try to re-establish the role itself. If he continues to lose the support of his parents and stops communicating with them, he often loses his successful role and takes on a failure role. A failing child usually chooses to give up in school and then often compounds his failure and further alienates his parents by taking drugs or engaging in promiscuous sex.

Parents have the difficult job of keeping in touch with their child and at the same time never implying that only they know best. They must support him and let him take responsibility for finding his goals. Support helps the child to be successful and secure in his role as a human being, and the support must continue even when the child falters or chooses a goal of which the parents do not approve. In this new society, the parent who stays involved, lets the child decide his own actions, helps him make a plan based on his decision, encourages the child to fulfill his plan, and does not excuse or punish failure will help his child. For the child to succeed, parents must not reduce their support.

Staying involved through thick and thin but letting the child choose is difficult for successful parents who obviously "know" better than the child what he needs. Although parents can say what they think is best and argue to support their conclusion, the child must judge and the parent must support his child's decision. The child's choices are never final. Parents and the child can talk honestly about his choices, and he can reevaluate his position and change. When parents give their opinions without pressure on the child to accept them, he may accept a goal the parents believe is wise.

Many parents believe that their child will gain a successful role if they provide him with material necessities and with love and support when they have the time, not when he needs it. They do not understand that the child needs to talk to and do things with them at times that may not be most convenient for them. A child accepts his parents' other obligations if they are discussed with him and if time is set aside for him.

Commonly, a child who lacks parental involvement slips in school. Parents who then withdraw further weaken the involvement. Parents just beginning to win the economic struggle and achieve a little security themselves may say, "I'm working hard. Why doesn't he?" Also, well-to-do parents who are very goal-oriented and interested in accumulating material wealth often think that warm, loving talk and play are unimportant; they, too, may fail to become involved with their children. Seeing no value in school because their parents have

communicated that school is the way to wealth, the children
see wealth as the road to more of the same loneliness they
now have. They take on a failure role. If the children become
involved with someone else, they may succeed as a person and
find a goal. Otherwise, financed indefinitely but unable to
become involved with their parents, they become chronic
failures.

Mark is the child of a successful father and a rather
devoted, concerned mother. Mark did well in grade school,
average in high school, and poorly in college. Associating
with friends his parents disapprove of and occasionally using
drugs, he works sporadically at becoming a rock musician. In
growing up, Mark had almost every advantage. Family
finances were a little tight when he was young, but from the
time he was five until now when he is approaching twenty, his
family has had few financial worries.

Mark's parents believe they have made it clear to him that
their hard work and dedication to their family brought about
the family's comfort. They believe it is clear to him because
it is so clear to them. They have worked hard and still do.
Mark, however, has not got the message. Seeing that he has an
easy, enjoyable life and that his parents seem to enjoy giving
him things and opportunities, he thinks he is doing them a
favor by accepting what they give him. In a sense, he is doing
them a favor because it is mostly through Mark that they
gain the role reinforcement they need now that they have
security. Although he may give lip service to goals, he is
primarily involved in finding his role; the idea of working
hard to achieve a goal that will, in turn, reinforce his role
does not occur to him. Smart enough to fake his way through
junior high school with fair grades, he paid little attention
and gave little thought to the future. During the last two

years of high school, when the work became more difficult and he thought about the hard work of college, he slacked off. Not wanting to go to college but thinking he had no choice, he tried to get out of college by making a poor record in high school. Although he had a role, it gradually became the role of failure because it had no good reinforcement. When Mark graduated from high school, it became suddenly obvious to his parents that he had no goals. In response they withdrew their emotional support and, gradually, their financial support. They broke their involvement with him, an involvement that was never strong because it was based partly on what they had given him rather than on what he had done for himself. Breaking the involvement undermined Mark's last chance for a successful role, leaving him with failure as his only choice. Totally dejected by his failure, his parents considered it a betrayal to them, a lack of appreciation for the hard work that provided the luxuries he enjoyed.

The source of the problem for Mark and most other children unable to achieve a satisfactory role for themselves as young adults is the home. Although parents provide many opportunities for their children to gain successful roles, they make few attempts to help the young child tie his early good feeling about himself to reasonable goals that prepare him for the goals he will need later in life. The parents become upset because he does not work hard in high school, even though they still gain satisfaction seeing him enjoy himself. Later, as the child wanders aimlessly through college, they become increasingly dissatisfied and withdraw their support.

Affluent or not, to raise successful children in our role-oriented society we must help them find goals that support their roles. If they do not succeed early, we must continue to support them in the hope that, with our continuing support, they will eventually find a goal that will reinforce their role. If we spend money for music and sports lessons, we must also spend time with our children encouraging them to work hard at what they are doing. We must guide them to the role reinforcement that success in achieving a goal provides. The child must learn that hard work is valuable to him as well as pleasing to his parents. It is bad to give a child many opportunities and then ignore him. Unless he is very talented and has great success in what he does, his parents' lack of interest in him will cause his feeling about himself to deteriorate. As his role as an independent, valuable human being slowly crumbles, he will lose interest in his activities.

In *Schools Without Failure*, I have described how children fail in school because schools deny that the child's humanity is primary. They say, "Work hard for goals and then we will reward you," rather than, "We will get to know you first and then encourage you to work for goals." The child, without goals at home and without a role at school, becomes frustrated and accepts failure early. Failure at school, even with success at home, may cause the child to develop a failure identity because school failure can greatly damage the child's belief in himself as a valuable, independent human being. Parents, therefore, have the additional, difficult job of helping their child be strong enough to succeed in an impersonal, goal-oriented school. Any time a child begins to fail in school, he may discover that other school failures pay attention and relate to him. They may suggest drugs, delinquency, or sex as ways to reduce the pain of failure. The child gains the unsatisfactory, painful role of a failure.

Parents must not only see that their child has an opportunity to gain a role through their support and acceptance, but they must also encourage him to work for a goal he believes will reinforce his role. As the child struggles to attain a goal to reinforce his role, parents must accept his choice even if it is not the goal they would have chosen for him. Goals vary; a child may choose one of a thousand different goals. Successful roles—the sense of oneself as valuable, respected, and cared for—are about the same for everyone. Failure roles are much more variable, exhibiting the variety of behaviors that I have described in Chapter Three. Because a person with a failure role cannot work for a success goal, it is pointless for a parent to concern himself with the child's goals if the child identifies with failure. To say to a failing child, "Stop loafing and start working," is a waste of breath. The parent must first become sufficiently involved with the child to help him change his role from failure to success. As the child becomes successful, the parent may also suggest achievable goals to help the child reinforce his feeling of success. Parents must have enough faith and patience to support and guide the child toward finding a goal that will reinforce his role. Parents who do so will avoid many of the problems described in this and the next chapter.

School

What can a parent do when he finds his child doing poorly in school, either failing or not working up to his ability? If he no longer thinks he can succeed in school, he has become an in-school dropout. Going to school because he must—there is little else for him to do—he puts no effort into his work and brings home failing or near-failing grades.

At age thirteen Susan is not involved in drugs, nor is she excessively interested in boys. Although she has a few friends and enjoys some of the school activities, especially the social life, she has given up performing in school at a level commensurate with her ability. Susan is in the eighth grade in a fairly standard school. Her goal-oriented school will not help her gain a successful role. In elementary school Susan did well because she became involved with teachers that she had all day and because subject matter was not too important. In the sixth grade, when grades became more important, she started slipping. More and more discouraged in the seventh grade, by the eighth grade she was hardly working at all. She brought home a poor report card, many unsatisfactory notices, and some comments from teachers saying, "Susan just does not try." Although she sometimes talks back to teachers, she is more often sullen and withdrawn, staying out of the teachers' way. When she talks about school, she says, "It's lousy, and I can't make it there." In school she is a failure.

Her parents must talk to her and do things with her that allow her to think of herself as a worthwhile person, respected by them. She must regain the feeling that her failure identity has caused her to lose—she has a successful role just as a human being. If her parents can help her gain a successful role, she may begin to do some of the hard work needed to succeed in school. Success in school will, in turn, reinforce her successful role. The longer anyone fails, the harder it is to help him to succeed. Because she has failed for a year and a half rather than having the four or five years of solid failure that cause children to lose all motivation to try in school, it is still possible for Susan's parents to find a way. Although both Susan and her parents know that she has the ability to succeed in school, she complains that school is boring, that the teachers are drags, and that the subjects mean nothing to her. Asking why she would put up with the whole irritating school business, she repeats her complaints whenever her parents bring up the subject of school.

Initially, I suggest that her parents say nothing about school.

It is hard to say nothing, because they are afraid that if she does not buckle down now, she will be totally unprepared for high school and college. Although at this time college is more their goal than hers, she also says, in a depressed tone, that she would like to go to college. She admits she has to succeed in high school to succeed in college. Susan would like to go to college because she thinks college may be better. Not tied to a strict schedule, students can choose their classes and have more chance for an involved social life. Still, although she says she has to work harder to succeed now, she is not doing much. The effort, the planning, and the interest are just not there.

Susan has the skills to succeed in junior high; she can read, she can write, and she can do enough arithmetic. When a family friend who knows nothing about her school progress visits her home and shows interest in her as a person, she becomes stimulated and happy, a reversal of her usual sour disdain of her family. In the company of these occasional visitors, she is able to speak thoughtfully, but as soon as they leave, she reverts to her withdrawn, nonmotivated behavior. This change in attitude should be a sign to her parents that they ought to accept her more as a person and less as a poor student, that they stop putting pressure on her to succeed because the pressure is not working.

To help Susan now, her parents must show their interest with an honest talk. They may say, "Sue, we have been putting pressure on you. We think you believe that you have failed us with what you are doing in school. Maybe you even believe you've failed yourself. You say you don't care, and maybe right now you don't. You feel it's worthless and hopeless and you have just about given up. You probably are a little angry at us because we haven't tried to understand what you face in school. But, Susan, we would like to get across to you that we are concerned. We are more concerned about you as a person than we are about your school failure and how it affects us."

That is the basic message that Susan's parents must get across. They should say it several times, even if Susan does not seem attentive. At the same time, they should stop pressuring her so she recognizes that something is indeed changing. When Susan starts to listen, there is a chance to help her. Her parents must tell her that they love her, want to talk to her, and want the best for her. Telling her in friendly ways that regardless of her present failure in school they still care, they must also say that upsetting as her failure is to them she is the one it harms most. They have to point out repeatedly that regardless of what she does in school she is their child and they will support her. "We love you, we would like to help you, and we're behind you, but success in school is your responsibility," must be communicated over and over. In a sentence, the message is: We care about you for your sake, not for our sake.

Sue's parents are using the first principle of Reality Therapy: they are becoming personally involved. People cannot become involved with others if their involvement is based on what the other person can do for them. In the identity society, involvement means: I am interested in you as a person, but you must figure out what goals you want for yourself. Susan's parents should have been communicating with her on this basis all along. However, it is not too late to start now. With Susan in the eighth grade, this year may be the last time they have a fairly easy chance to become involved with her. Later on, if she has many more years of failure, they may need professional help.

Susan's parents must talk with each other and examine their own motivations, their own concerns, and their own goals. They must be sure they are not pushing Susan to fulfill their own goals, rather than allowing her and encouraging her to find her own. They may be advised to send Susan to a psychiatrist, but I believe they are better advised to find psychological help for themselves to understand better Susan's behavior. Talking with a professional person a few times may help them carry out the suggestions of this chapter.

Whatever Susan's parents do, they should agree and do it together. If you are Susan's mother or father and want to be friendly and involved with her, you must be nonjudgmental about her work in school at the present time. Do not go over her report card in detail and make her explain it. When you sign it and give it back to her, you may say, "Susan, I see this is what you're doing and there's nothing really for me to say. I have to see it and sign it, but I'm not that concerned with this particular report card. The eighth grade is not the end of the world for you or for me or for anyone else." Both true and nonjudgmental, this statement will help regain involvement. If you continually give value judgments, saying, "Well, that's wrong," or "That's not helping," or "I told you never to do that," or "You certainly shouldn't have done that," or "You know these things upset me," you will destroy Susan's desire to communicate her concerns to you. Believing she is being judged continually she will keep quiet and find her identity by failing in school and associating with other failing students.

When Susan believes that you care, which may be after several months, ask her to tell you a little of what she does in school. If she begins to talk about school, and she will if she knows you will not judge her, then you have communicated to her that you really do care. If Susan tells you what she is doing in school, and if you listen to her without making a value judgment, you can begin to motivate her to work. I suggest that you reread Chapters Four and Five to reinforce in your mind the necessity of approaching Susan nonjudgmentally. If she believes that you want to be involved with her and that you accept her for herself, she will begin to feel more successful. She will never feel more successful if she thinks you are judging everything she does.

Try to have short conversations with Susan. Do not try for long talks. Ask her briefly what she is doing and listen to her when she tells you. For a week, a month, or even six months if it is hard to get her started talking, just let her tell you what she is doing. If she is getting along poorly, be strong enough to let her suffer the natural consequences of her behavior. Be kind and considerate, as always, but do not give her special attention or sympathy because she has made some bad choices and suffers the consequences. Do not reject her, even if what she has done is hard for you to accept. After a time, Susan will talk more and tell more of what she is doing. When she does, you may begin to point out some alternatives to what she is doing that might be better choices. Do not tell her they are better; that is for her to decide. As she starts to think about alternatives, the involvement with her that you have lost will begin to be reestablished.

Telling you what she is doing will force Susan to evaluate her behavior. If you do not evaluate her behavior for her, if you do nothing more than ask her where her behavior is taking her, she will understand its natural consequences and necessarily make an evaluation herself. Her past evaluation of her behavior is that failure is the best she can achieve. You are attempting to get her to change this evaluation. Do not try to go too fast; if you do, she will interpret your anxiety as preaching and blame her failure on you rather than seeing it as the result of her behavior. You are trying to become involved with Sue and to use this involvement, as in Reality Therapy, to get her to evaluate her own behavior. She must begin to reject her irresponsible behavior and see that blaming you, even if you were somewhat at fault, is not helping her. You must learn to eliminate the long face, the preaching, the "I told you so," and the "I didn't do this when I was a child."

So far you have become involved with her, and you have listened to her nonjudgmentally. Next, gauging whether the relationship is strong enough to bear the stress, ask her, "Well, is there anything you're doing now that you believe you might do in a better way?" Initially, she may try to defend and justify her behavior, even though she knows that she is not helping herself. Do not look for a dramatic change because she is not too upset by her failure identity. After all, she has many friends who are failing and who support her attitude toward school. Say, "Sue, examine your behavior and see if it is helping you." Although you cannot avoid the intimation that what she is doing is wrong, you are now enough involved with her so that the intimation alone will not break the involvement you have gained.

Let her know there might be a better way open to her. You want her to begin thinking about alternatives and about judging her own behavior. She can understand that life has many instances that call for evaluation and planning to succeed. Help her begin believing that life need not be haphazard, that she need not live day-to-day, doing or not doing what she feels like. Rather, it is possible to evaluate options, plan a course of action, and take responsibility for your decision. To get Susan to make an evaluation, use variations of the question: Is what you are doing really helping you?

At this point, assuming that the involvement has become strong, she will not run away, get mad, or say, "See, you want me to be perfect and that's all you've really been talking to me about." Instead she may say, "Well, there are some things I might do to improve, but I don't know if I can. I don't think the teachers care. I've got so far behind in my skills that I don't think I can ever catch up." It is not true that she is too far behind. It is only an excuse to avoid hard work. In any grade in any public school, including the eighth, once she starts working, she can catch up.

If she mentions something she wants to do to improve herself that you do not think is a good beginning, do not say, "Well, I don't think you should do that; you should do this instead." Accept whatever she suggests as a plan to improve herself. Show that you are interested and that you support her. If you show disappointment, she will give up. A person deciding to change from failure to success needs constant support. Any move toward success will help Sue to become more successful. Success breeds success, and it does not really matter what the first success is. Too many parents think that a child should succeed along certain defined pathways that they believe are right. Abandoning this attitude may help Sue get started. Once she believes that she can be successful in any way, she is on her way to identifying herself as a successful person. Do not worry about what she is doing; just give her encouragement. Do not urge or exhort her now, even though you believe that if she would just work a little harder she might succeed readily. She has not much strength in working toward success, but she has a lot of strength and practice at working toward failure. Try to nurture what little success she has.

Sue discovers through the renewed involvement with you, her parents, that you are really interested in her and that she can succeed. You must understand that Sue was trying to make it on her own, even though she was using behavior that supported and reinforced a failure identity. She had neither a good involvement with you as parents nor a good involvement with teachers and successful students at school. Her involvement was with other failing students. An even greater involvement was her own misery. At thirteen, Sue was not yet involved with drugs or sex, more serious choices to reduce the pain of failure, but she certainly was involved in failure.

As the involvement continues and as she tells you what she is doing, especially about a little success, you must help her to make a plan. Up to now she has probably made only minimum plans. Once she begins to experience success, your help and guidance in developing a reasonable, long-term plan will reinforce her success. The plan should not be too complicated. Sue herself must be involved in making the plan, whether it is with you, her school counselor, her teacher, or her principal. Your talks with her will help her to be able to make much of the plan herself. You can use your knowledge of the world to help her, but the plan must be developed together. If it is your plan, Sue will not follow it.

When Sue starts on her plan, ask her for a commitment to carry out the plan. The discussion in Chapter Four suggests ways to get a commitment that Sue is likely to fulfill. The commitment may take any form, verbal or written, that you believe will help her do what she says she is going to do. For Sue to gain a successful identity, she must make a commitment to you or to someone else to carry out the plan that she has developed and that she believes will lead her toward success. After she makes the commitment, be patient.

If Sue fulfills her commitment, congratulate her. You may praise her a little more than seems natural because she has not had praise for a long time. Although the praise you give may seem excessive or even silly to you for the small amount of work she has done according to her own plan, it is not excessive to Susan. If she were older, perhaps seventeen or eighteen, she might be a little embarrassed by excessive praise. She might even say, "Shut up, you're overdoing it. I really haven't accomplished that much yet." Nevertheless she will enjoy whatever praise you give. Praise is always motivating; never worry that praise will lessen your involvement. On the contrary, it increases the involvement and helps solidify Susan's ability to make plans and to fulfill commitments.

What do you do if she continues in a lackadaisical way, does not follow the plan, and thus does not fulfill the commitment? Be patient, do not accept excuses, and do not punish her. If she tries to give an excuse say, "Don't excuse yourself; it's not necessary. Just do what you say you are going to do as soon as you can." Punishment will immediately destroy the relationship you are trying to build. People cannot become involved if one person hurts the other. Keep trying to work out a reasonable plan and get commitments from her to do what the plan states. When she has attained her goal, she will become more secure in her new role of accepting herself and of being involved with you. The involvement will be increased because she realizes that you accepted her as a human being before she started to accomplish her plan.

As Sue starts to succeed, you must maintain your involvement with her. You cannot return to the kind of nonrelationship that contributed to her failure. Keep the relationship going; talk to her, listen to her, reinforce her as a person, encourage her, praise her. Changing from failure to success takes a long time. Sue may take two steps backward for every three steps forward. Be patient and understand that it is not easy for her to find a goal that reinforces her new belief in herself as a worthwhile human being, her belief that she now has a successful, independent role. Because she has had much failure, success in school will come slowly.

When you first realize that Sue is having trouble in school, go to the school and talk to a teacher, counselor, or administrator. Find at least one person in the school who will take some interest in her and who will try, even though he has only moments (only moments are necessary to help a girl like Sue) to do with her in school what you are trying to do at home. In the beginning she will not succeed in every class, and it is not necessary that she does. She has been so negative to school that work that ordinarily interests girls her age does not interest her. Some special attention will help. Ask a teacher to talk with Sue to find some work that Sue will do because it is presented personally. Then encourage Sue to do it and give her praise when she succeeds. This start will raise her interest and more will come.

In addition to following my suggestions for becoming involved with and guiding Sue and for encouraging one of her teachers to do the same, you might take a third step: find a tutor in the neighborhood. Do not look for a professional teacher or a professional tutoring service. Instead, find someone in the community to whom Sue can relate, someone a little older than she such as a high school or young college girl or, perhaps, a young college boy whose attention and interest in her school success might flatter Sue. First the tutor will spend a few hours getting acquainted by talking about her interests and how school may relate to them. Then he can begin helping Sue directly, although each session should be devoted to talk as well as tutoring. In my experience, parents who have followed my suggestion of obtaining a qualified young person as a tutor have almost always found that their child has been greatly helped.

Do not give your child much help with his homework—too much irritation and antagonism occur, and too many old scenes repeat themselves. It is better to hire someone else. Parents who cannot afford a tutor can sometimes find someone free of charge if they call a local college. Many students volunteer for tutorial work to needy young people. The important qualities to seek in a tutor are warmth, a sense of humor, and school success.

In helping Sue become successful at school, you have not played the know-it-all, the judge, the preacher, the successful person, while she played the failure. You have let her work and succeed in a very important part of her life. You have neither defended the school nor allowed Sue to use the school as an excuse for her failure.

The above comments are not addressed particularly to one parent or another. This paragraph is specifically for fathers. Working hard to provide good homes for their families, many fathers do not seem to have much time for their children. But to help a child like Sue, her father should spend some time, at least half an hour a week, exclusively with her. They should do something together in which she can experience some success. Perhaps they go shopping for mother. Sue's father can let her make the selections and then reinforce her choices; the parents having already agreed to accept whatever she chooses. Sometimes a little success with a girl's father produces what appears to be a miracle.

As a further aid to success, both parents can help Sue succeed around the house. Give her a job she can do and pay her for doing it. Parents will find that successful children will be glad to do housework for nothing; failing children, however, often need the extra reinforcement that money provides. Encourage Sue to spend her money for something she enjoys, and accept her purchase even if it is something you do not approve of, such as an unintelligible (to you) rock music record. Criticism will hamper her chance of identifying herself as a thoughtful, successful person and lessen your involvement.

A parent who follows the suggestions of this chapter—develop involvement, get the child to talk about what he is doing, ask the child to make value judgments and plans, get commitments, and neither excuse nor punish—will help his child and start him along the road to success in school.

Chapter Seven

Failure in Children: Drug Use and Sex

Drug Use

More dramatic than school failure are the many problems associated with a child taking drugs. The wide publicity given to drug use has generated the growth of many groups that try to help children using any of the many drugs that seem so readily available. Synanon, Daytop Lodge and Phoenix Houses, youth houses, religious retreats and free clinics, Hot Lines, school programs and radio and television programs all try to help prevent further drug usage and get current users to give up drugs. This chapter describes specific steps a parent can take if he discovers his child uses drugs.

Accepting the moderate use of alcohol and tobacco by adults, most parents are not greatly concerned if their adolescent child smokes or takes an occasional drink. As a child approaches legal age, parental concern about drinking is small. The police mirror this attitude by rarely prosecuting minors for drinking. Drug use by children of any age, however, is unacceptable to parents, regardless of how permissive they are. Even parents who do not drink or smoke and strongly disapprove of drinking and smoking are more tolerant of such practices than of drug use.

Although the full effects of many drugs are still unknown, some agreement derived from the mass of information available on this emotional subject does exist. Recent information shows that habitual use of marijuana, smoking many cigarettes daily, may so reduce a person's drive that he does little except sit around, but an occasional marijuana cigarette, perhaps two or three a week, has little or no effect on a person's normal functioning. Marijuana aside, there is good evidence that heavy or even moderate use of barbiturates, amphetamines, cocaine, morphine, heroin, LSD, and mescaline drastically reduces a person's ability to function effectively. People who use these drugs usually increase the amount and find it very difficult to stop. Fortunately, most people who use drugs never go beyond using marijuana and eventually limit themselves to marijuana in small amounts. It is incumbent upon a parent who discovers his child using drugs to find out the amount and type of drug the child takes. A parent may not like his child to smoke an occasional marijuana cigarette, but it is much better than using stronger, more debilitating narcotic drugs. Heroin, LSD, and the amphetamines (especially Methedrine) do the most harm physically and mentally to the individual.

Although penalties against the use of marijuana may be decreased, legalization appears unlikely. Even if we discover marijuana is less harmful than alcohol, it will remain illegal because many people consider it to be a pathway to failure. Whether or not marijuana is a pathway to failure is open to conjecture, but in any case our legislators are now so overwhelmed with trying to deal with failures that they will not soon take what they believe to be a potentially dangerous step.

Many states are reducing the charge for possession of marijuana for personal use to a misdeameanor because making felons out of users creates more harm than the actual use of the drug. Legal or illegal, because it is readily available and generally less harmful than other drugs, marijuana will continue to be widely used and will cause fewer problems than any other common illegal drug.

If a child who functions (a recent study reported that 10 percent of high school honor society presidents have smoked marijuana), does well in school, gets along at home, has some reasonable goals, and works toward them is found smoking a little marijuana, what should his parents do? Responsible parents who get along well with their child would necessarily be concerned because they would fear that failure or frustration outside the home would lead the child to increase his use of marijuana to relieve the pain of failure. Furthermore, the frequent use of marijuana may result in the child's arrest; a felony conviction on the child's record will make it difficult for him to achieve many desirable goals in life. Although many judges reduce a first offense to a misdemeanor or throw the charge out completely if the young man or woman is relatively responsible, no parent can count on leniency. Should the judge wish to make an example, he may send the child to prison for smoking or possessing marijuana or, in some states, for being around those who are using it.

A parent who discovers that his child is smoking marijuana should not call the police. Although the parent does not condone the child's breaking the law, he believes that not calling the police (for what the child usually believes is a harmless habit) is a better choice than doing so and thereby destroying his involvement with his child. The parent must—and this is difficult—communicate his concern to a child who is often responsible in other ways. Probably his son will become defensive when he finds that his parents know he smokes marijuana; he does not want to alienate them over something he believes they do not understand. Because the confrontation is difficult, the parents should avoid a bitter "the world's coming to an end" scene. Rather than argue, they should calmly and briefly discuss with him that their concern is not so much for the marijuana as for his breaking of the law. If the parents respect the law, if they do not drink or smoke heavily, and if they are interested in and involved with their child, they may be able, by their own example, to persuade their son to smoke less marijuana or stop altogether.

The life you lead and your relationship with your child are all you, a parent, have going for you, but they may be enough. Arguments that marijuana is dangerous will not work, nor will threats of calling the police. If your child is otherwise successful, your involvement with him will help him to stop smoking marijuana or at least to cut down on his smoking and be careful to avoid arrest.

If you break your involvement with your son, his chances of trouble are greatly increased because he will become careless. He may wish to be caught to show you he now feels failure and hurt you for the part he believes you played in his failure. Children who start to fail often fail more if their parents make an issue over whatever they are doing and thus weaken the involvement. It is better to be cool about marijuana and warm toward your child. The parent might suggest, although it is illegal, that his son join him in the good fellowship of a before-dinner drink and introduce him to the enjoyment offered by the moderate use of alcohol. Although minors cannot legally drink liquor in most states, the penalties are less severe for the use of alcohol than for the use of marijuana.

Except for drunk driving, drinking is always a misdemeanor, but use of marijuana is often a felony. In addition, the police usually enforce the laws against marijuana much more vigorously than they do the laws against minors drinking.

A less common but more pressing problem faces parents who discover their child of twelve or thirteen starting to experiment with drugs. Judy is a bright, personable, somewhat bratty, spoiled thirteen-year-old. Recently she had been less open than usual and was sometimes depressed and sometimes exhilarated. Her mother discovered some capsules in Judy's purse and told Dad. When they confronted her, she told them blandly that she had been a "user" of uppers (amphetamines) and downers (barbiturates) for the past four months. She said that although she had been curious for some time, it was not until she read the illustrated color folders distributed in school giving detailed information about drugs that she decided to search her parents' medicine cabinet to see whether they had any of the ones mentioned. She found some yellows (Nembutal capsules) and sampled some. Not liking the effect, she asked around school and found a seventh-grade boy who had some uppers, Dexedrine, that he traded for her downers, Nembutal. By stealing the Nembutal and some of her mother's prescribed Valium, a common tranquilizer, she was able to trade for uppers, which she took frequently for four months. The pills caused her erratic mood swings.

Judy was not upset by her parents' discovery because she had decided to convince them she was desperate and must continue to have drugs; the capsules she had were the last of her supply. In a dramatic follow-up to the first discussion of her use of drugs, she told her parents she was hooked on uppers and asked them to get her a moderate amount legally through the family doctor. She wanted to show them she was a big girl who was a real "user." If her parents had been foolish enough to indulge her by persuading the family doctor to give her some pills, she would have been in a powerful position in her social clique at school as someone with a legal supply who had conned her parents. When her parents refused, in one scene after another, she threatened everything from burning down the house to suicide in her effort to force them to yield to her. Knowing they would not call the police, when she made her initial demand she half-expected them to swallow her claim that she was hooked and give her drugs to keep her quiet.

Judy's parents should flatly refuse to get her any drugs. Both to keep drugs from Judy and to set a good example, they should remove all the drugs from the house, including tranquilizers and sleeping pills. Parents without enough incentive to stop using pills themselves have trouble helping their daughter. Finally, and a very important point, they should not discuss drugs with her on any occasion; despite what they might have learned, they know little about the realities of taking drugs. If, after discovering she cannot get drugs, she says she will stop all drug use except a little marijuana, they should make no comment. If she persists in trying to discuss drugs, her parents should say that they do not use them and that they know nothing about them except that they are illegal. This approach will not work with an older child, but it sometimes works well with a young, unsophisticated child who has little access to drugs and who does not enjoy the effect of the drugs herself as much as the effect her use of them has on her parents.

At the same time, her parents should work hard to establish a warm, friendly relationship, to encourage her to have friends over, and to keep involved. If she tests them again by drinking from the parental liquor supply (a common event in this pattern), they should lock up or get rid of the liquor and say nothing. If her parents can live through a few hysterical weeks, a girl like Judy will usually calm down. She may still say she uses pills and pretend to be loaded, or she may occasionally use them and obviously be under their influence at home. If Judy's parents do as I have suggested, they can ignore these episodes because they will almost always become less and less frequent. If Judy is failing in school, her parents can help her by following what I have suggested in Chapter Six.

As much as parents are concerned over the previous problems, they become frantic when their son or daughter seems to disintegrate completely under the influence of drugs. Stan, at nineteen, has smoked marijuana for many years, has taken all kinds of pills (uppers and downers), has injected Methedrine (speed) into his veins, has tried LSD and mescaline, and has been so unstrung on Methedrine that he has taken heroin intravenously to control the effects of the Methedrine. Having tried a little of everything, Stan now stays clear of LSD and heroin, but he still shoots speed, takes many barbiturates, and smokes a great deal of marijuana. Stan lives a drug life; his only work is dealing in drugs to assure his own supply.

Although Stan sometimes feels the pain of failure, he is usually so anesthetized by drugs that he feels little except the relief from pain that they provide. Because for him drugs have replaced everything else, he is not aware that his life has been reduced to a series of disconnected experiences under their influence. Occasionally, large doses or new combinations of drugs provide him with the pleasure of quick and unexpected relief from his loneliness and failure. At such times he rationalizes that drugs give him a level of psychological consciousness and a feeling of awareness that he cannot gain otherwise. When he is not completely under the influence of drugs, however, he is aware of little except pain and the feeling that life without drugs is futile. Stan has retreated into a drug-induced numbness.

Meetings with old friends are brief and never satisfying. Stan associates only with young people like himself who rationalize their self-involved behavior in many ways. At the beginning of his drug life these associates, not friends, give him the illusion of involvement. As he becomes more and more involved with drugs, his involvement with such associates lessens. He begins to realize that people on drugs offer little lasting or quality involvement and that he is alone with drugs as his only companion.

Under these circumstances a parent must regain enough of Stan's confidence to start some communication with him again. A young person completely involved with drugs usually has only slight contact with his parents. His parents know he takes drugs because he told them so when he moved out of the house, adding that drugs had solved all his problems. Blaming them for his previous problems, he told them of his drug use to hurt them and show them he had taken on the mores of the antisquare drug society. Stan has long hair and dresses in a uniform of various old clothes. Taking pride in his lack of personal ambition and goals, he seems relaxed and at ease. He is conforming to his chosen society, which dedicates itself to drugs and ridicules the square values. There was probably much friction and antagonism when he left home. His parents have told him that he is not welcome in their home as long as he takes drugs, hangs around with his drug friends, dresses as he does, and refuses to work.

If you, as a parent, have said this to your son—and many parents have—retract it. Tell him you were wrong; tell him that whatever he has done he is welcome in your home. The only condition to this welcome is that you do not want him or his friends to use drugs while they are under your roof. If he must use drugs, he can do so somewhere else. Tell him that as long as he is at home, whether for an hour, a day, a week, or longer, you will neither discuss drugs and his activities nor judge what he is doing now or has done in the past. Your only condition is that he cannot use drugs in your house.

Many parents doubt they can get a son like Stan to come home. His return is possible because, as much as he says he does not want to come home, he will find that the drug world is a transient, unstable life with little welcome anywhere unless he shares drugs with others. The search for drugs keeps him constantly on the go. Sometimes when he has no money and his friends will not give him any, he cannot get drugs. At these times, without the anesthesia the drugs provide, the pain associated with Stan's failure identity becomes acute. If you can keep in touch with him, you will sometimes see him when he is suffering from acute pain because he cannot get drugs. Your offer to let him come home will then look good to him.

If he comes home, even for a brief period and even though you do not believe he deserves the attention, act as you would if he were not on drugs. Ask him to observe reasonable standards of cleanliness, serve him good food, see that he is comfortable, and be as pleasant as you can in talking with him. In your conversations do not talk at all about drugs or the drug world. While staying at home, he may say that home is the last place he wants to be, that he is there only until he pulls himself together and goes back with his friends, that he is just stopping over on his way north or south, or that you should not think he is going to stay because you have made him welcome. If he is exposed to any lectures, threats, or wailing about his past and present behavior, he will probably leave. Keep the conversation light and refrain from self-indulgent complaining. In the beginning, it is important to make Stan welcome and let him know he can stay as long as he wants.

Many parents are completely out of touch with their child; even if they want to do as I have suggested here, they do not know where the child is. In my experience, most children want to keep some contact with their parents. If the parent tells the child's friends, places an occasional ad in the newspaper, or calls one of the organizations that trace children, the young person can almost always be found. The parent may have to go into the part of the city where he thinks his child is and tell people that he is interested in getting in touch with him. In most cases, contact can be made and an invitation to return home given.

Assuming Stan is found and will come home, he will stay home for longer and longer periods if he finds comfort, no preaching, and good food, and if his friends are welcome provided only that they forgo drugs and maintain reasonable standards of cleanliness while in your house. After he is home awhile, he will want to talk to you seriously. These first conversations are very important. You must learn to listen nonjudgmentally for long periods as he tells you his rationalizations. He may ramble at length about experiences and plans that make little sense to you because, like everyone, he must defend his choice of a way of life, failing or successful.

You must also understand that because he has taken large amounts of drugs his mind may be affected for a long time. If he has taken LSD, he may appear to have brain damage because he cannot follow any subject for long and seems a stranger to himself. Six months to a year may be necessary if he has taken a great deal of LSD, but eventually this detachment will pass providing he gets good food and sufficient rest. Although I do not believe that LSD causes permanent brain damage, it certainly can affect the brain for a long time. Regardless of what drugs he used, Stan will probably talk frequently. You must listen to him despite the incoherence of some of his conversation. If he asks you a question, give him an honest, short, nonjudgmental answer. Listen with interest, and recognize that even though you may not agree with him, he has a right to say what he is saying. Without being obvious, let him know you are glad he is home.

If Stan wants to talk to a brother, a sister, an aunt, or a grandfather, they should converse with him the same way you do. He needs someone to listen to him nonjudgmentally for long periods while he reestablishes the idea that he is involved with someone who cares about him. You are beginning to rebuild a successful identity by giving him the feeling that he is important enough to be listened to by people who will not run him down. People are beginning to replace drugs.

Let him stay home doing almost nothing for a long time. He may just lie around the house, listen to his records, talk with his friends when they come by, or spend time with you. Do not suggest he do anything more. Wait until he starts to do something or he asks you about doing something. This period takes strength on your part. You will say to yourself, "Well, now that he is off the drugs, he ought to get going." You must realize, however, that his identity was almost totally one of failure for a long time and you are still rebuilding the beginning of a relationship that will allow him to succeed. Almost like reraising a child, it takes much time and strength on the part of the parent not to hurry.

There is a possibility that Stan might read this book and say triumphantly, "See, you're just doing what the doctor said; it's not really what you believe at all." Do not deny you are taking these suggestions. Just say, "Well, it seems worth a try to me. I wasn't satisfied that we never talked before," and (if applicable), "I'm sorry I practically threw you out of the house. What I did was wrong. I want you to be welcome. I like having you here." If you can say this honestly, Stan will probably be satisfied because he is trying to determine that you care. As a psychiatrist, I have had experience with many young people like Stan who have faced me with a similar complaint that my only interest in them was the money their parents paid me. In response, I said that I did care about them, and usually this was enough.

Next, the parent must find someone outside family or friends to help Stan. It is difficult to know when to do this. Good signs are that he has stopped using drugs, he is willing to stay home, he has accepted you, and he may be ready to do something besides lying around the house. He needs a good relationship with someone with experience with people like Stan who can help him make some value judgments about his life, both past and future. Ordinarily, the parent cannot confront Stan with his behavior to get him to make a judgment. As soon as the parent does, Stan thinks he is preaching, even if he is not. He may again start taking drugs to show that his parent should have left him alone.

The person Stan talks to must be someone who Stan feels has an open attitude toward him as a person who has taken narcotics. He might be a psychiatrist, a psychologist, a social worker, a minister, or a community worker with experience with people like Stan. He might be someone who runs a small halfway house, a settlement house, or a youth house in the community. Stan may decide to move to a place such as Synanon where he can have the day-to-day support of others who have also decided to try to start life again without drugs. He needs successful involvement with others to strengthen his identity, which had started to move toward success while he was at home. Synanon, Daytop Lodge, or Phoenix House will probably help Stan more than any individual can. Such places provide a program tailored to the drug user's intense need for personal involvement. They also provide him with opportunities to work in, and then out of, the house. Such institutions are available in many large cities and some smaller towns. If Stan can be guided from your home to one of them, it will be a big step forward. If, however, he is comfortable at home, if he has stopped using drugs, and if he is talking with you, just getting him to talk to someone outside the home, such as a therapist, may be enough. You can try either suggestion first. If it does not seem to work, try the other. Whoever tries to help Stan must be patient. If he is comfortable at home, there is time for him and his parents to work out what he might do next. Both Stan's parents and whoever else is helping him can guide him toward working for a goal of his choice—going back to school, taking a job, or, in the beginning, doing volunteer work.

Of course Stan will have setbacks. Sometimes he will become upset because his parents are acting in a warm, involved, noncritical manner. He wants them to go back to their old ways so he can rationalize his urge, arising from doubt and loneliness, to start taking drugs again. He may try to hurt his parents or he may try to get them to preach at him or throw him out of the house so he can again say he has nothing in the world to depend on except drugs. Parents must expect to be tested continuously and must live patiently through these down periods. For a son who has taken a great many drugs over a long period of time, rehabilitation may take as long as five years. It took a long time for Stan to get there, and it will take a long time for him to come back.

Sex

Several different kinds of sexual problems confront parents with increasing frequency today. One problem is the pregnancy of a daughter. For most families, this is an emergency that requires a quick decision. Parents need guidance both on what to do and on how to do it so their daughter learns something and handles herself more responsibly in the future. One way a girl can receive recognition, the feeling that she is involved and worthwhile, is through sexual relationships. Today many girls over fifteen who are failing in school find the opportunity to become sexually involved with a boy. A single standard of sexual conduct (discussed in the following chapter) for both girls and boys stating that sex without commitment is all right is accepted by many men and women of all ages. Thus most failing girls see little or nothing morally wrong in getting involved with sex to reduce the pain of their failure.

Jodi has been going with Tom for three years. Both seventeen, they are about to graduate from high school. With a poor school record, Jodi has neither preparation for a good job nor desire to continue in school. Half-heartedly she says she might go to a secretarial or cosmetology school. Her relationship with Tom is all that prevents her from feeling failure, but she believes that this relationship is very good. Tom cares for her and she feels good knowing him and knowing that her parents like him and welcome him in their home. Jodi and Tom have been sexually intimate during their senior year, and now, about five months from graduation, Jodi discovers she is pregnant. Having a fairly open relationship with her mother, she tells her she suspects she is pregnant. Jodi does not think the world is coming to an end, nor does she think her parents will throw her out. Rather, she has faith that her mother and father will help her work out this problem.

Jodi is surprised to discover she is far from sure she wants to marry Tom now. The pregnancy has forced her to examine the depth of her involvement with Tom. Almost every one of her friends who married at seventeen or eighteen after becoming pregnant is unhappy. Now realizing that her involvement with Tom is not the kind she believes would lead to a successful marriage, she begins to feel failure. She becomes depressed and her school work slips even further. Her parents, confronted with a situation that calls for some action, do not understand her relationship with Tom and do not know what to do.

How should Jodi and her parents solve this serious problem? Some parents try to get an abortion for their daughter.

In recent years, forced marriages among young people have become unpopular. Because marriage in this society must support identity, forced ones rarely work. Such a marriage often lasts only a year or two; after the divorce, the woman is left with the baby, sometimes two babies, little financial support, and much loneliness and misery. The man feels upset, but he can recover with little encumbrance. The woman has the responsibility for the child, which she may or may not choose to take. In any case, many parents believe that marriage is not a good choice. The woman can keep the baby, give it to her parents, put it up for adoption, or see that it is raised in a foster home. These are poor solutions for the baby unless

good care is available. Unmarried women today, at Jodi's age
and older, consider these various alternatives. Unless they have
religious scruples, most women choose abortion as the best
solution open to them. This decision is now possible in all
states because of the recent Supreme Court ruling upholding
the right to abortion.

Whatever choice the family makes, how the parents help
Jodi regain a successful identity is most important. Because
sexual pressures on young women are extremely high, parents
must accept the likelihood that their daughter, successful or
failing, will have sexual relationships prior to marriage.
Young women in our society are depicted by the popular
media and by advertisements as valuable largely for their
sexual potential rather than their human potential. Therefore,
it is difficult for a girl to be accepted by a boy without having
a sexual relationship with him. Many girls, not wanting to
be sexually involved, find themselves unable to have more
than casual relationships with young men. The social pressures
on young men to be sexually intimate are great also. Going
with a girl and refraining from sexual activity in the face of
all these pressures is rare.

Because the Pill and other methods of birth control are not
easily available to women under college age, and rubber
prophylactics are not easily obtainable by young boys, many
young women become pregnant accidentally. Others become
pregnant even if birth control is available to them because
they feel failure; pregnancy is reassurance that they are at
least fulfilling their female role. Another reason a young
woman becomes pregnant is to test her family's involvement
and support, to see if they will stand by her in difficult times.
Like many girls, Jodi probably was affected by all three of
these factors. Jodi's parents must understand them all to help

her make the best plan. Concerned as much with the future as with the present, they must help solve the problem without alienating Jodi. If they can build a strong relationship with her in which she feels she can be successful without marrying now and that the pregnancy has not ruined her life, they may help her gain the strength both to solve the immediate problem and to develop enough responsibility not to become pregnant again before she marries. If they concern themselves only with solving the problem at least expense to themselves in terms of their relationships with each other, their friends, and their family, they may lose Jodi.

Jodi needs to be made welcome at home. Whether she chooses to be married, to keep the baby, to have the baby adopted, or to have an abortion, she needs her parents to help and stand by her. After discussing the alternatives with her, Jodi's parents must tell her what they believe is best and allow her to make her own decision. Her parents' support will help her find the strength to make a reasonable decision. If she wants advice from someone with experience working with other pregnant girls, she might talk to a minister, a doctor, a psychiatrist, a social worker, or a school counselor. Whoever Jodi talks to should urge her to make a decision quickly, for although Tom and his family may be included in the discussion, the primary responsibility is Jodi's. If she is going to learn something, she must make her decision and then make a plan to live by it reasonably. The particular decision she makes is less important than carrying out what follows from it. Once she makes a decision, her parents must continue to support her. If Jodi receives good guidance and makes a decision that her parents help her implement, she will probably regain her successful identity.

A daughter who is sexually promiscuous poses another

common problem for parents. The woman is young, perhaps sixteen to twenty years old. Having sexual relationships with a series of men, perhaps more than one at a time, she does not believe that sex is in any way coupled with commitment. Jan, seventeen years old, uses sex for recreation and for control of men. Usually she will prostitute only to get money for drugs. Although she demeans herself as a person in her own as well as her family's eyes, there seems to be no way to stop her from continuing to choose a life of sexual promiscuity. With a serious failure identity and having had little success in her life, the one success she can count on is her ability to attract men into sexual relationships.

Jan uses sex for the same purpose as Stan uses drugs: to reduce the pain of a failure identity. Whether or not she also uses drugs, she can be treated in the same way that Stan was. First, get her to come home. In her life away from home there will be times when no one seems to want her; if home is made attractive to her and she is welcomed without preaching, she will return at one of these times. See that she is checked for venereal diseases and receives medical treatment if she has one. If she does not want to call or see anyone and prefers to sit around the house and watch television, let her do so for a while.

Accept Jan as your daughter; your only request is that she not indulge in sexual activities or take drugs in her own home. As with Stan, try slowly and carefully to show her that you care for her. Do not discuss her sexual exploits, but listen non-judgmentally if she wants to talk about them. Because promiscuous sexual behavior is easier to give up than habitual drug use, Jan can probably get a fresh start without seeing a therapist. If she stays home and seems to give up her promiscuity, her mother will probably become sufficiently involved with her to suggest she go either back to school or to work. To help her refrain from sexual activities for a while, she needs her family, not other young people in similar circumstances as did Stan. After she settles down, and girls like Jan usually stay close to home, a therapist can help her rearrange her ideas about men and sex. Because the family involvement is critical to her giving up her promiscuity, however, it should precede any help from a therapist.

Promiscuity in a very young girl, perhaps twelve or thirteen, is a much more difficult situation. At age thirteen, Linda is out of control. She stays out nights, goes away for weekends, associates with older people, hitchhikes, and seems willing to have a sexual relationship with almost anyone. As much as her parents try, they cannot get her to stay home for more than a week at a time. She rejects everything except her idea of the free life. For girls like Linda I recommend calling the juvenile authorities. The parents can do nothing themselves, and there are almost no private institutions that can help girls like Linda. The parents' best hope is that their city has a good juvenile home with a program that can help them again become involved with their daughter.

Certainly Linda will resent being in custody; she will say she hates you and will berate you as the ones who caused her to be locked up. If the juvenile hall is fairly good, if you visit her regularly, and if you tell her that you did not know what else to do to keep her from running wild at age thirteen, she will usually understand—sometimes only after several years of custody and probation—that you do love her and are trying to care for her. As she grows older and believes you love her, you may help her reenter school. She may have to be enrolled at a new school because her reputation is too bad at her local school. As she leaves her wild, promiscuous life, you must be tolerant of her choices of clothes, music, hairdos, and friends. Accept these if she will stay home, and treat her as I have suggested in the examples of Stan and Jan. Linda needs a professional therapist to help her work out a plan for a better life. Whether she sees the therapist in custody or as a condition of probation, many visits will probably be required.

Parents interested in helping their child will usually find that cooperative juvenile authorities want to work out a reasonable plan for their daughter in custody to prepare her for going home. If Linda understands that she is being sent home as an alternative to staying in custody, she may stay home and give up her promiscuous behavior. If her parents do not make demands of her, they may be able to become reinvolved with her. To rehabilitate Linda is difficult. What I have suggested takes a long time and may not work, but any attempt to treat her in a less structured way, allowing her to continue her self-destructive behavior, may be disastrous.

Psychological Problems

Less common in the identity society than children with the problems discussed in this and the previous chapter are children in psychiatric difficulty. The child is not acting out, running from home, using drugs, engaging in sex, or failing seriously in school, yet he is obviously out of touch with some or all of reality. Because young people in our society can act in many ways to try to relieve the pain of failure, they are much more likely to have problems related to school, drugs, or sex than to have psychiatric problems manifested primarily by withdrawal into themselves. Nevertheless, the latter still do exist.

With young children, say under age ten, I believe it is best that parents who observe their child withdrawing into himself get professional psychological help. The parents must learn to become involved with the child so that he can regain a successful identity. They might bring the child to the therapist with them once or twice to make sure he understands the problem and can suggest ways for the parents to guide the child toward involvement. In addition, a good nursery school will help the child get involved with other children and return to reality. If the child's parents receive professional help, many nursery schools will take children who are obviously disturbed. For a child of public school age, a good private school that specializes in involved education can be helpful. At this age, a tutor is another good alternative.

An older child, say between ten and twenty, with psychiatric problems is often helped by visiting a therapist without his parents. The child may have some involvement with his parents but no friends. Seeing a therapist, joining a young people's group, or both are valuable methods for helping this child. Although the parents may visit the therapist occasionally, he is primarily seeing the child. Old enough to understand the value of a relationship with the therapist, the child can be helped if the therapist is skillful at becoming involved with children and thereby reducing their loneliness.

Although in the minds of many people therapist means psychiatrist—a medical doctor specializing in psychological problems—competent therapists can also be found among psychologists and social workers in private practice. In addition, a parent who actively searches within his community can usually get help from community clinics or agencies at little cost. The parent should find a therapist who is warm and whom the child likes and enjoys seeing. At first the child may need a little urging to see the therapist, but if the therapist is competent, the child will probably want to see him after a few visits. If the child resists for a long time, the parent should discuss with the therapist the possibility of changing therapists. A therapist may recommend a psychiatric hospital for some disturbed children who need more help than can be obtained in outpatient treatment. This rare occurrence is beyond the scope of this book.

Sometimes, if the child is only slightly withdrawn from reality so that difficulty with his school work is his only problem, and if the parent still has moderately good communication with him, a good plan is to get the child a tutor. The tutor should be a warm-hearted high school or college student who likes children. To give the child the friendship he needs, the tutor will spend an hour or so with him once or twice a week under the pretext that the child needs academic help. The tutor will provide involvement at much lower cost than a professional therapist can. A nonprofessional tutor will be of little help to a child severely withdrawn. For a moderately withdrawn child who needs involvement outside of his family, however, a warm tutor can be an effective aid.

Chapter Eight

Sexual Behavior

Men and women who have experienced joyful sex will go through the proverbial fire and flood to enjoy more of its pleasure. Fearing that the pleasure of sex will distract people from working hard and respecting authority, those in power, including parents, religious leaders, and politicians, have for centuries attempted to restrict sex to marriage and to create an atmosphere in which sexual pleasure is considered wrong. They believe that if people, especially young people, discover the joy of sex, they will devote too much time pursuing this role pleasure, time better spent in goal-oriented activities. No evidence, however, supports this belief. On the contrary, a pleasurable sexual relationship helps most people build a successful life and allows them to devote time and energy to the pursuit of responsible nonsexual activity. Those who do not enjoy a good sex life devote time and energy to excessive preoccupation with sex.

Although the need for a good sex life is more accepted in the identity society than it was in the survival society, many people have not learned to utilize this acceptance to find sexual satisfaction. That many people are actively searching for a good sexual relationship is clearly shown by the unprecedented sales of popular books containing information about sex and advice to those seeking more enjoyment from sex. The inability of so many people to find a good sexual relationship is, I believe, directly related to their failure to gain a successful identity. Unsatisfactory as their search for a good sexual relationship is, most people who identify with failure continue to search in the hope they will sometimes succeed. Although part of their motivation is biological, the need for involvement is the principal drive, as it is for all people. They know that a sexual relationship implies the chance to become involved. Thus lonely, uninvolved people are urgently and continually attracted to sex because it seems to be a simple solution to the problem of getting involved.

Sexual attraction moves people toward involvement even without immediate culmination in a sexual relationship. People who are sexually attracted find that intellectual and social activities are more enjoyable when they are together. Just walking and holding hands with someone you care for can make all the world around you more alive and exciting. A time comes, however, when the relationship must culminate in a sexual embrace or the magic will be lost. The age at which a sexual relationship should occur is less clearly established in the identity society than it was in the survival society, in which being old enough to marry was the generally accepted age. In some social classes, marriage itself was required to make a sexual relationship permissible. Now, however, regardless of what we say directly to him, each young person decides for himself when first to engage in a sexual relationship. He will base this decision, as he does all decisions, on his confidence in himself and on what he has learned from those who are involved with him. The more successful he is, the more rational his decision will be. If he is a failure, he may make an unreasonable decision about sex as one of a series of unrealistic decisions that will dominate his life.

Many involvements have nothing to do with sex. If they are warm and worthwhile, as in a good friendship, a good job, or a good family, they can help overcome the pain that is always a part of life without a good sexual involvement. Although sufficiently good nonsexual involvements may enable a person to identify as successful, it is difficult to gain a successful identity without a good sexual relationship. The difficulty is illustrated by the many Catholic priests who do not wish to leave the church but who also do not wish to remain celibate, arguing that they would be more effective if they were allowed to marry.

Rarely, however, is the obstacle to finding a good sexual relationship an externally imposed sanction, as it is with priests. The obstacle is within us. From earliest childhood, we have been taught that sexual pleasure is wrong and in some way dirty, and we are continually admonished against touching our own or viewing anyone else's sex organs. A child taught these attitudes must unlearn them later to enjoy sex.

The emphasis on the immoral aspects of sex most often affected people in the middle echelons of the power hierarchy because they had some security and thus had something to lose by being labeled immoral and perhaps punished. Hester in *The Scarlet Letter* wore her "A" to protect someone who had more to lose. Because those in the lower echelons did not threaten the power hierarchy and had nothing to lose anyway, they were allowed much sexual freedom as long as they stayed in their place. Sexual license for those who desire it has of course always been part of the reward for being at the top of the power hierarchy.

As our moral view of sex changes in the new identity society, we are reducing our adherence to the traditional double standard of sexual behavior. According to the double standard, an unmarried man can have sex either with or without commitment with little social disapproval, but a woman can have sex only with commitment. Commitment almost always means marriage. Although a woman can have sex without marriage when it is not legally possible for her to marry, she must be involved and ready to marry as soon as she can.

The double standard, which seems on the surface to be unfair to women, would not have been tolerated by women for so many years had they not gained some advantages by accepting it. Women willing to deny themselves sex until marriage were assigned a higher value by men in the marriage market. Because until recently most women needed marriage for security, they felt a strong incentive to keep their value high. Men needed marriage for several reasons. First, it provided steady sexual gratification. Second, men needed marriage to have children and thus increase their security; children not only contributed to the family income, but they were also the only social security for old or disabled parents. In developing countries today, birth control often fails for this reason. Third, in the middle and upper classes married men were socially more acceptable. Even in today's identity society, to be alone is socially less acceptable than to be married. When men wanted to get married, they married women of higher value; thus, keeping chaste until marriage paid off for women.

In the survival society marriages were more stable than they are today because men and women recognized both that divorce was a serious threat to the security of the whole family and that a family was the best means of satisfying one's need for involvement. Marriages were not more stable because they were sexually more satisfactory than are marriages today; probably they were less so because of the prevailing moral attitude that even marital sex was wrong if it was excessively joyful. With the security of the identity society, the need to stay married has decreased. When marriages dissolve now, there is more security for all of the members of the family and less social stigma than there was. Therefore, couples often divorce if the marriage does not provide good involvement and a satisfactory sexual relationship. Although the survival society was socially more stable than the identity society because fewer marriages ended in divorce, it was much more painful for lonely, sexually frustrated men and women locked into unhappy marriages.

When a man and a woman live together, married or not, their sexual relationship is an important indicator of the degree of involvement they have achieved as a couple. If sex is good for both, usually their total involvement is good. If it is bad for one or both, each often questions all of his involvement with the other. A few people report that even though they have lost enough involvement to get divorced, their sexual relationship remains good until their final separation. In these cases sex is usually much more enjoyable for one partner than the other; the one who still enjoys the sex denies reality for short periods, hoping the lost involvement will be regained. This partner usually has no one else at the time and dreads the idea of divorce and being alone.

Some couples unable to achieve a good sex life do not realize, because they are afraid and ignorant, that sex may not be a valid measure of their involvement. They may fear sex because they have been told it is bad. Even if they do not fear sex, they are generally too uncomfortable talking about it to learn the simple facts of how to satisfy each other. Their sexual involvement may be worse than their other involvement; good sexual counseling would improve their marriage.

Fear and ignorance about sex are more detrimental now than they were in the survival society because today a premium is placed on good sexual involvement. Many couples who cannot find a satisfactory sexual relationship constantly question their marriage. If this questioning occurs for a long time, and especially if one or the other finds or believes he can find a better sexual partner, a couple will divorce.

Nevertheless, many couples without a good sexual relationship stay married. Although sex is not satisfying for them, constantly testing and threatening their relationship, they do not separate for many reasons: security, children, social or occupational position, or other parts of the marriage involvement that may be good. Moreover, they do not believe they will find someone better. To reduce the pain caused by their unsatisfactory sexual relationship, they rarely have sex together. They may escape in short- or long-term affairs, which may be somewhat satisfying, but the couple involved or someone close to the couple who can adversely affect them always considers these relationships immoral. People either suppressing sex or engaging in an affair they believe is wrong may suffer from psychological or psychosomatic symptoms to replace the sexual involvement they have lost. As I have described in Chapter Three, the symptoms, while painful, give the person a degree of involvement with himself and thereby reduce the pain of the poor sexual relationship. In addition, the psychological symptoms may gain from the partner attention and care not possible without the complaint. Thus, although the person has little sex, he may gain personal attention.

In the identity society, however, most people have been so deeply affected by the premium put on sex as a means of pleasure for both men and women that few couples, married or not, stay together when their sexual relationship is so bad that the couple rarely has sex together. Believing that sex can be an intensely pleasurable and varied experience, they think that anyone who misses giving and receiving this pleasure is foolish.

Today many people, especially the young, the affluent, and the educated, are abandoning the old double standard for a new single standard stating that sex without commitment (specifically without marriage) is all right for both men and women; the couple, however, must be involved with and care for each other. The new single standard applies only to unmarried people. Adultery is still considered immoral for both men and women. Implied but not always realized in the single standard is the condition that, unless there is an explicit understanding to the contrary, sex without commitment may lead to a commitment.

In any society a few people engage in sex not only without commitment but also without involvement. Today, these few receive a disproportionate amount of publicity that makes their conduct seem both more desirable and more widespread than it is. Their number is few and is probably no greater now than it was in the survival society. Considering that more people are now searching for involvement, their number may even have decreased.

To justify our change from the traditional double standard to the new single standard, we have developed a rationale that may eventually become a new morality. I believe that the rationale can be stated as follows: "Because marriage is no longer necessary to provide security for either men or women, a couple should not marry unless they love each other and until they are ready to commit themselves to each other. A decision as serious as marriage should not be made without knowing whether the couple is compatible sexually, socially, and intellectually. The time to marry, therefore, is when both people feel the pressure of total involvement and a willingness to commit themselves to each other, not just the pressure of sex, which can fool them into thinking there is more involvement than really exists." The new rationale continues: "Because sex exerts a pressure, both social and biological, it should be relieved early in the relationship so that the couple can, for at least six months, more easily learn about each other in many ways—social, economic, and intellectual—not related to sex. The tension produced by sexual frustration in a man and a woman attracted to each other should be dissipated for both of them; a couple should not decide to get married to relieve their sexual frustration."

People who identify with success can find sexual involvement and commitment with the new single standard. Neither standard, old or new, will help people who identify with failure find a successful sexual relationship. People who are involved and feel successful think it makes little sense to defer sex as they enter into a new relationship. If the relationship does not work out, they suffer no more than a brief intense pain, since they are not totally dependent on this one relationship or on the sex in it for their successful identity. As everyone is, they are shaken by rejection, but they are not defeated. With enough confidence in themselves to continue looking for another good, loving relationship, they will not settle easily or quickly for less.

Sometimes a person with a failure identity who enters into a sexual relationship is able to find involvement with the help of a kind and mature partner. Such a relationship can be a powerful force to help the person toward success. This point is beautifully illustrated in Robert Anderson's play *Tea and Sympathy*, in which a young man who feels personal and sexual failure is helped toward success by a sensitive woman who accepts him both sexually and as a person. In other cases, a person enters a relationship believing he is successful but needing more involvement to solidify that belief. He needs a loving sexual involvement to gain more strength and more success. If he becomes involved, gives a commitment, and then is rejected, he can lose his successful identity and fail. Sex works both ways; it can be a powerful determinant of both success and failure.

A failing person drawn to sex because it promises involvement often gains only brief physical relief. Involvement continues to elude him. Becoming more lonely and withdrawing further into failure when he sees that sex does not lead to involvement for him, the failing person may begin to rationalize and deny that good sex and involvement necessarily go together because for him they rarely do. From the sexual propaganda that surrounds us in the identity society, he may well infer that sex without involvement is sometimes enough because it reinforces his hope that he will eventually find involvement if he is successful in finding sex. He will then doggedly pursue sex for its own sake, not realizing that he loses rather than gains involvement as he does so. Although he thinks he is doing his best to get involved, his failure increases. A vicious cycle is created: the more he pursues sex, the more failure he feels because he has not found involvement. The more failure he feels, the more he pursues sex, hoping to gain involvement, but involvement will elude him because he is more interested in sex than in his partner as a person.

Although everyone is reached to some degree by the commercial sexual propaganda of all the media, its financial success depends on lonely frustrated people. Unable to find human involvement, they become involved with sex itself. They may read about and see movies about sex and look at sexy pictures. The sexual material is called pornographic if it is not related to warm human involvement. Similarly, men who use prostitutes to satisfy their sexual urge are not involved at all. Men who have known some involvement sometimes find a regular call girl who gives them, if she is good at her trade, the illusion of involvement with no strings attached. Because these men depend on the girl for more than sexual relief, prostitutes who give some warmth and involvement have no lack of patrons. Many men and women unable to satisfy the need for involvement try to anesthetize the pain with drugs. Heavy users of alcohol and other drugs have little or no sex life; the involvement with drugs and alcohol replaces the need for sex.

Whether or not they practice the new single standard, most people marry when they become sexually, socially, intellectually, and often economically involved because they want to make a long-term commitment to each other and, usually, because they want children. After marriage, as they learn more about each other and mature in the sexual relationship, they continue to enjoy sex with the partner they love. They also learn that sex, like any long-term relationship, is more enjoyable at some times than at other times. Like those who enjoy a drink or two to help them be more convivial, they enjoy a sexually stimulating movie, book, or play or sexually suggestive jokes to enhance their sexual feelings and perhaps lead to more enjoyable lovemaking. Although they do not need the stimulation to urge them toward involvement—they already are involved—the stimulation provides them with a good sexual feeling that can intermittently heighten a committed sexual relationship. Puritanical restriction of all sexual material penalizes successful people who enjoy mild stimulation.

Many popular books that attempt to tell people how to obtain a good sex life do not consider whether the reader has a failure identity or a success identity. These books do not help failures because a good sex life requires more than the ability to perform according to instructions. A successful identity is needed to develop a warm, involved sexual relationship. In Chapter Five I described ways to rear a chid that will lead to his developing a successful identity. To review briefly, a child is most likely to develop a successful identity in a family in which the members, adult and child, love and are committed to each other, in which the mother and father hug, kiss, and hold each other and their children, and in which the children are taught that a sexual relationship is part of love. In addition to a loving family, as preparation for a good sex life a child needs friends both in and out of school as well as a good school in which he learns and succeeds by talking, playing, working, and achieving intellectually.

Learning to talk and listen, to appreciate what other people say and do, is excellent preparation for marriage. A common cause of marriage failure is a breakdown in the couple's ability to communicate thoughtfully with each other about topics of mutual interest. Although their sexual involvement may be good, neither person reinforces the other as an intelligent, worthwhile person. Because talking and listening are vital to any involvement, when they fail, the man and woman both become lonely. Even a good sexual relationship cannot overcome this pervasive loneliness. As the man and the woman lose involvement with each other, their sexual relationship usually gets worse also.

Men and women must find the most effective way to use the new single standard to reach a commitment to each other. Some couples enjoy a sexual relationship without commitment and with the understanding that their involvement will never lead to a long-term commitment. No problem need arise if they discuss the situation so that both the man and the woman clearly understand that their relationship is limited to a good involvement, with no promised commitment beyond the week-to-week sexual relationship.

Many women, having adopted the new sex-prior-to-commitment single standard intellectually but not yet fully accepting it emotionally, tend to give and expect more commitment than the standard provides for. When there is no specific understanding with the man that there is no commitment—or sometimes even with such an understanding—a woman may suffer severe rejection when he leaves. If the commitment is one-sided, either by the man or by the woman, the one who gives the commitment and does not get it in return will feel failure. The couple's involvement will then deteriorate rapidly.

In my psychiatric practice I have seen many young unmarried women who, accepting the single standard, have engaged in a long-term sexual relationship with a man. Although he had made no commitment to them, they saw him exclusively and had no desire for anyone else. Attempting to practice the single standard before they understood and accepted all of its implications, they did not realize the need to get either a commitment or a clarification that there was not going to be one. A girl such as this was enjoying her boyfriend socially as well as sexually. Deeply involved, she hoped the involvement would lead to a commitment between them. As the relationship continued, sometimes for several years, the man often became less rather than more willing to make a long-term commitment. The single standard gives the man every right to take the uncommitted position. Aided by their experience that there are more available women than men, men are often socially and sexually secure enough to practice the single standard exactly as it is stated. Although many women try to practice it and seem to succeed for a while, they usually want a commitment at some time. When the reality of the man's noncommitment dawns on them, they become much more upset than they would be if they truly accepted the single standard. Honest with neither themselves nor their partner, these women are often hurt.

My discussion of the new single standard does not suggest that I personally either advocate it or advise against it. Attempting to clarify the attitude of many people today, I claim neither that everyone has accepted the single standard nor that they should. Whatever its acceptance, I would like to offer two suggestions to women who say they do accept the single standard.

First, if a young woman wants a commitment from the man with whom she is having a long-term affair, she must plan a course of action. Obviously, a woman should be as attentive and as attractive as possible during the relationship, and she should insist from the beginning that the man be the same. But if she does not get a commitment from him, that is, if he does not state that he wants to be with her indefinitely, married or not as she wishes, she must make a plan to force the issue. She should decide to break the relationship if she does not get a commitment from him within some specific time period. When that time limit is reached, she must be strong enough to separate despite the pain. If she does not get a commitment shortly after the separation, she never will. The young woman may either keep the plan to herself or tell the man about it, depending on which choice she thinks will better motivate him. She should not give him an open ultimatum if she fears she would be overwhelmed by the pain of an immediate rejection that an ultimatum might cause.

In any new relationship, the involvement increases up to a point and then levels off or perhaps diminishes slightly. The woman should ask for a commitment at the time she believes the involvement has reached the peak. If she does not get a commitment, separating at this time will emphasize the involvement at its maximum. Certainly I understand that a woman finds setting and adhering to a time limit most difficult. Knowing that the relationship will deteriorate rapidly if she does not do so should help a woman gain the strength to follow through. If she does not muster the strength to hold the time limit and instead continues to temporize in a haphazard involvement with little commitment, the affair will end bitterly. She will have wasted valuable time that could have been used to find someone else. I do not believe only one man exists for any woman. Those who believe this nonsense are opening themselves to much suffering if the "one and only" man is lost.

My second suggestion for women who accept the single standard is to take a new single-standard approach to dating as well as to sex. To compete on more equal terms with women who follow my suggestion, women who still believe in the old double standard might also consider adopting this new approach to dating; they can do so without giving up their standards about sex. An advantage of women in the survival society, in which the double standard was generally accepted, was that they would eventually be dated seriously by a man who would ask them to marry if they remained passive and did not engage in sexual relationships. A woman's family and friends, as well as marriage brokers, all helped to find men who would date her. Because a woman did not take the initiative, however, if she was not dated, she could do little but accept being an old maid.

In the new single-standard society which we are now entering, men still take the initiative by asking women out and courting them. Accepting this dating tradition, most women have not thought much about taking the initiative themselves. I believe that a woman willing to have sex without commitment can give up her passive, date-me-I'm-here attitude and take the initiative in starting an involvement. Not needing the double standard to make herself marriageable, a woman today is foolish to sit and wait for a man to call her or use various indirect methods of meeting a man such as asking friends or relatives to introduce her.

Formerly, women lost value in men's eyes if they took the initiative because their initiative was interpreted as a sexual invitation. Now, when a man knows that regardless of who makes the first call, a woman accepting the single standard will enter a sexual relationship with him if good involvement develops, it makes little difference who makes the first call. The woman must make clear to the man that her initiative does not promise a sexual relationship. As long as she lets him know that sex is a separate decision, she will retain full value in the new single-standard society.

A girl who discovers an attractive man she would like to meet should take the initiative by asking him, either directly or by dropping him a note, to meet her for lunch or for an after-work coffee or cocktail, or perhaps to come to her house along with a few other guests. She is protecting herself against an unpleasant first meeting by having a few other people present or by limiting the time so that she can excuse herself easily if she wants to. If the man accepts her invitation, she should provide her own transportation to their meeting place. During the first meeting she should act much as she would have if he had asked her out. She should not apologize for or discuss her asking him out. If he asks why she took this unorthodox step, she should say only that she wanted to meet him. After the first meeting, the girl can decide whether or not she wants to ask the man again. The change in courtship I am suggesting is no greater than other changes already made in sexual behavior. If the man and woman are attracted to each other, their relationship will not be affected by her having taken the first step.

Marriage in the identity society requires that the couple be sexually, socially, and intellectually involved. While respecting the other person's wishes for time for some separate activities, both husband and wife must look for various activities that they enjoy together. Even the best sexual relationship is not enough by itself to sustain a lifelong involvement.

Husbands and wives should understand that few marriages are fifty-fifty in terms of making decisions. In most marriages, one person is dominant; he may make 60 or 70 percent of the decisions. Most friendships are like that, and there is no reason for marriage to be different. If one partner expects equality and finds dominance, he has found the usual; it is equality that is unusual. Although a reasonable inequality is rarely a reason for divorce, the understanding that one partner will probably dominate is necessary to prevent the other partner from struggling for an equality that is rarely possible. Although many marriages stay together even when one person makes 80 or 90 percent of the decisions, I doubt that these marriages can be called successful.

Many couples remain together long after their marriage has failed. The force that holds them together is their mutual involvement with the misery of the marriage, as I have described in Chapter Two. Each partner settles for what he thinks is the lesser pain of the marriage rather than the greater pain of divorce. An example is a marriage in which one partner is an alcoholic. Assuming the man is the alcoholic, he is dominated and denigrated by his wife, who at the same time faithfully supports him. He settles for the pain of being degraded to avoid the greater pain of being left alone. His wife, who seems to get almost nothing from the marriage except the misery of living with a man involved with alcohol, does get the pleasure of her martyrdom and her self-proclaimed superiority over him. Both of them believe they would rather be involved with the familiar misery that reinforces their failure identities than divorce and lose this reinforcement.

Some couples with little involvement and little desire for each other socially, intellectually, or sexually nevertheless stay together. A bland lack of interest replaces the love and friendship that have dissipated. Rarely is there hate; when there is, the couple usually divorces. By each partner's finding his own interests and going his own way, many couples with no interest in each other stay married. They do not divorce because they are not miserable and they believe that the arrangement they have may be as good as any they are likely to have with someone else. Knowing each other well and trusting each other in a certain way, they are not bound to each other with either misery or love. Another reason that keeps them from divorcing is that they are ashamed of their failure and do not wish to admit it to the outside world. In cases such as this, the couple usually has children. If the parents are not constantly fighting, maintaining the home may be good for the children.

A few suggestions may be helpful for people who start dating after a divorce or after ending an unhappy love affair. Talk as little as possible about your previous husband or wife or your previous boyfriend or girlfriend. Always a good rule, it is essential when you first meet someone new. If the urge to talk is overwhelming, as it may be, limit your story to one good session and say little more from then on. Because your previous relationship was a failure, if you talk much about it, the person you are dating will see that you had some part in causing the failure. Although a worthwhile discussion about life that may strengthen a new involvement sometimes stems from talking about the past, such a discussion should move from the specific failure of the past to a more general and, hopefully, more optimistic view of the future. If you wish to talk about your life, emphasize your successes rather than your failures. To build a good new relationship, stay in the present and point to the future. Do not complain about your present life to someone you care for, and beware of other people who dwell on their troubles. Nothing hampers involvement like complaining.

On dates, be warm, personal, and friendly. Do everything possible to get involved. Talk about what you do, and do things together worth talking about. For instance, if you go to a movie or a play on a date, tie your feeling good to what you did and how your being together helped you enjoy the evening. Plan something of interest for dates. Rather than just hoping everything will go smoothly, suggest interesting places and activities to share. A good involvement will develop more easily if you have something definite to do and talk about than if you just have dinner and go home to bed. There is nothing wrong with good conversation or good sex; however, to build the involvement that may lead to commitment, sharing some activities is helpful.

In dating be open-minded. Although your date may not fulfill your expectations, if he or she has some redeeming qualities, try at least twice if you are given the chance. Much loneliness may have made him bitter, but companionship and acceptance will cause him quickly to become more attractive.

Chapter Nine

Criminal Justice,
Hospitals, and Welfare

Our society has three major institutions to deal with chronic failure: the welfare system, hospitals for the chronically ill, and the system for criminal justice. At present there is agreement that these institutions work poorly. Only rarely do they provide more than bare survival, which in the identity society is not sufficient. They house or serve those who are lonely, who have identified with failure, and who are involved with themselves and their own misery. In these institutions persons have little chance to change. Even if we are largely successful in raising children who identify with success, there will still be some failures; we must treat them so that they have a chance to become successful. To do so, we must begin now to apply, when we can, the principles of Reality Therapy to the institutions that deal with failures. Where these principles cannot be applied because of custom and because of the inertia common to large outmoded institutions, we must either change the institution so that the principles can apply or do away with some institutions, such as mental hospitals, that are probably beyond hope of reasonable change.

Almost everyone agrees that the present welfare system

perpetuates failure. Although the Nixon administration did not wholeheartedly push the plan and Congress rejected it, the Family Assistance Plan was a way to begin to break out of the pattern of continual failure. Sooner or later this or similar proposals will become law and be tested against the requirement that, to succeed, a welfare plan must help people to become involved and then motivate them to work when jobs are available. The Nixon proposal did not pass this test, but it was a first step in a direction that may eventually produce a workable plan. Just keeping people alive, with little chance for involvement or worth, as we do now, is locking them and most of their children into failure at a cost to the society greater than the cost of changing the system. Some suggestions on possible ways to improve the welfare system are made in the next chapter. Specific plans are beyond the scope of this book.

Hospitals for the chronically inadequate, physically as well as mentally, can be improved more easily than the correctional system can be improved because there is no moral opposition to changing our hospitals as there is to changing our correctional procedures. In the hospitals we continue to do what we do for many reasons, all of which were valid to someone in charge at one time; if we want to change them, however, we can do so without fear of being attacked because those in our care have committed no crime. And hospitals are staffed by doctors, nurses, and rehabilitation workers who would like to do a better job but who are handicapped by outmoded medical and psychiatric tradition.

Much of what has to be done in the so-called mental hospitals was described in Chapter 4 of *Reality Therapy*, as long ago as 1965. Further ideas applicable to mental hospitals and, with little modification, to hospitals for the chronically ill are offered in Chapter Three of this book. We must give up our inaccurate psychiatric and medical labels and the often harmful traditional treatment that follows from them and understand that people choose to become disabled or to stay disabled psychologically or physically when they identify as failures. If the failure is not treated, the symptoms, physical or mental, will persist indefinitely. Although vigorous treatment of some symptoms may produce temporary relief, they will usually return or others, physical or mental, will take their place. The lonely, failing patient must be given a chance in the hospital to become involved with other patients, with the staff, with outside successful volunteers, and with his family. With the motivation gained through this involvement, he must have opportunities to develop worth, first in the hospital and then in a program out of the hospital. Dr. G. L. Harrington's pioneering work on Ward 206 of the Veterans Administration Neuropsychiatric Hospital in West Los Angeles in 1963 and 1964 showed that the program outlined in this book could be implemented successfully. Although Dr. Harrington developed a successful program in the hospital, he was not able to extend the program outside the hospital; therefore, once a patient left, he lacked assistance in maintaining successful involvements and getting a job. An outside program would have helped the men progress in their rehabilitation.

Reducing the emphasis on physical symptoms and rejecting totally the concept of mental illness, we must reject the idea that for many chronic organic symptoms medical treatment is primary. When some medical care is needed, it should not extend beyond the minor role it plays in most chronic disabilities. The importance of the identification with failure, stemming from lack of involvement and lack of worth, that is channeled into a physical or mental disability must be recog-

nized. Although our present inadequate and medically dominated hospital system attempts to deny it, chronic disability is
more a social than a medical problem.

The remainder of this chapter will focus on the correctional
system, which includes probation, parole, jails, reformatories,
and prisons. Despite wide recognition that the correctional
system is not only ineffective but that it is also a school in
which mild failures rapidly learn to become serious or chronic
failures, it will be especially difficult to change the correctional
system. Unlike welfare and hospitals, where inadequate knowledge and outmoded tradition are the stumbling block, the
correctional system resists change because of the ancient
"moral" belief that crime must be punished. Correctional reform does not occur primarily because we do not accept that
crime is almost always a product of failure, that in our correctional system we punish failure, and that the punishment
of those who fail only drives them further into failure. If we
can view criminals as failures more than as people who must be
punished, we can change the system to give them a chance for
success, an option that our present system denies. To do so
requires both legal changes and realization that revenge and
retribution do not contribute to rehabilitation. In this chapter
I suggest some changes in legal procedure that do not totally
abandon punishment but call for its use much less frequently
than now. In making these suggestions, I will introduce the
concept of the Community Involvement Center, a concept discussed more fully in the next chapter.

The correctional system handles the people who break the
laws of our society, people poorly served by a philosophy of
justice that was inadequate in the survival society and is more
glaringly inadequate in the identity society. Few people in the
identity society commit crimes to survive, such as stealing

food for a starving family. Most criminals (other than traffic offenders) fall into two groups. Those in the first group, who make up less than 20 percent of the criminals, attempt to overcome a sense of failure through money gained by holdup, burglary, larceny, embezzlement, and swindling.

Almost all of the remaining criminals attempt through alcohol, drugs, prostitution, gambling, vagrancy, or disorderly conduct to escape from the pain of their failure. Few in the second group, except drug users, ever commit crimes of the first group. Drug users, who usually commit nonviolent robbery and burglary, would commit fewer of these crimes if they could be helped to stop using drugs. A third small group, few of whom are apprehended and convicted, comprises the racketeers and professional criminals; they do not think that what they do is wrong or that they are failures. For them, breaking the law is part of their work, and many of them have a successful identity in their own social group. Because they often have powerful connections, both in the police department and politically, they are usually acquitted or receive a light sentence when they are caught. A small proportion of all criminals are those in a fourth group, those who commit crimes of passion. Nothing will ever stop these crimes. When they are recognized, our present punitive system treats the offenders less harshly than it would had they committed the same crime without the motivation of passion.

Most of the people in our jails and workhouses (not prisons) are criminals in the second group whose mode of failure, such as drinking and drug usage, causes them to be arrested and convicted often. Involved with failure and pain as a constant companion, when they drink or use drugs to get rid of the pain they care little about what happens to them. For them, crime is not failure; failure is crime.

Most prison officials recognize that 85 percent of the men in custody are not dangerous. They are lonely, incompetent failures whose only "success" is breaking the law. Despite their talk about getting out and making good, they are so habitually involved in failure that almost all of them honestly see no other alternative. They spend much of their adult lives in a series of correctional facilities. Judges see the same people over and over again, alcoholics being the most notorious chronic repeaters, as well as an increasing parade of new offenders each year. Once convicted, unless they get probation, they are sentenced to a jail, workhouse, reformatory, or prison that almost always firmly reinforces failure in each inmate. More than 400,000 men and women are warehoused in overcrowded prisons across the country, prisons that, with rare exceptions,* breed only failure, antagonism, and hostility.

As recently as 1969, the Presidentially appointed National Committee on Violence reported:

> Prisons and correctional facilities operate in isolation and reject public scrutiny. Programs of rehabilitation are shallow and dominated by greater concern for punishment and custody than for correction. Prison inmate work assignments usually bear little relationship to employment opportunities outside. Internal supervision is often inadequate. Correctional administrators are often said to be presiding over schools in crime. Jails are often the most appalling shame in the criminal justice system, notoriously ill managed and poorly staffed. Scandalous conditions have been repeatedly reported. The jails have been indicted as crime breeding institutions.

A large police force and prosecution system has been established to enforce the criminal laws through arrest, trial, conviction, and sentencing of lawbreakers. Despite this apparatus, many professional racketeers escape arrest through

---

* Tehachapi, a California Department of Corrections prison, seems to be one of the exceptions.

corruption. In addition, wealthy criminals who are arrested are often acquitted through the work of lawyers whom the poor cannot afford. The few wealthy criminals who are convicted are recognized as most likely to succeed in any rehabilitation program and often get probation.

One reason why people are sent to prison is that every society feels that wrongdoing should not be overlooked. Doing something reduces the chance that people will take the law into their own hands.

The poor and the inadequate people who fill our prisons are sent there in the usually vain hope that three goals will be accomplished: (1) punishment will cause the criminal to reform, (2) society will be safe when he is locked up, and (3) severe punishment of some will serve as a deterrent to others contemplating crime.

Starting with goal number one, let us examine each in detail. Why punishment does not accomplish reformation has been amply explained in this book, especially in Chapters Three and Four. Sixty percent of those in custody over eighteen years of age have been there before. As I have stated earlier, when a man who identifies himself as a failure is punished, his failure identity is reinforced. He will tend to behave in the same way that led to his initial incarceration and usually spend more and more time in custody as he grows older. Therefore, the assumption that punishment will cause a person to change his behavior and become rehabilitated is completely wrong.

Goal number two holds that if a person is caught and punished, society will be protected from him during his period of imprisonment. Except for possible lawbreaking by his family that may be related to his absence, society is generally protected while he is locked up. When he is released, however, as his identification with failure grows he will probably be more dangerous to society because he is more hostile, more incompetent, and less able to support himself. Almost always, he is more of a burden to society after his imprisonment than before. Because we obviously will not imprison all criminals for the rest of their lives, the imprisonment that occurs is, at best, of temporary benefit to society. Even though prison population is rising, society is not safer, because there are enough new criminals each year who, when added to the hostile people released, more than make up for any safety provided by an increase in prison population. The belief that the existence of prisons increases our safety is seriously disputed by a California study* that shows that of 60,000 crimes of personal violence reported in 1966, only 1,700 adult offenders were committed to prison. Jailing these few criminals (3 percent) could not add much to our safety.

Goal number three argues that if we imprison some people, others who may feel temporary failure and be tempted to crime will be deterred because they do not want to risk arrest and prison. How often this deterrent effect occurs is not known. Perhaps swift, sure, impartial punishment is, as many criminologists suggest, a deterrent. If one understands the identity society, however, it is clear that punishment and the security of prison are attractive to people who identify with failure. The punishment confirms their failure, and the security of prison both ensures their survival and reinforces their failure identity. Therefore, unless our society can prevent people from growing into maturity identifying themselves as failures and expressing hostility against those around them as their particular form of self-involvement, the deterrent effect of punishment, even severe punishment, will be of little value. The

* "Crime and Penalties in California," published by the California Legislature in 1968.

California report flatly states: "No authority can be found to support the value of severe penalty policies as deterrents for the majority of offenders." The deterrent effect of punishment works well for people who identify themselves as successful but who, under stress, are tempted to commit a crime such as embezzlement for personal gain. Although they may be temporarily short of money or they may feel temporarily isolated and uninvolved, their overall identity is that of success; thus, if they see that people are arrested and convicted, they are unwilling to take a chance and commit a crime. Punishing others, however, has little or no effect on most people who commit crimes. They are so involved with themselves and with failure that they pay little attention to the consequences of their acts.

If, as I have argued, two of the three assumptions about punishment are not true and the third, that punishment may be a deterrent, is valid for only a few people, what can we do that is more effective than what we are doing now?

First of all, we must reexamine carefully what we call crimes. Earlier in the chapter I said that for many people, their failure—drunkenness, drug possession and use, vagrancy, chronic gambling, disorderly conduct, and sexual offenses—is a crime; when they are caught, the law designates them criminal, compounding their failure. A book that should be heeded, *An Honest Politician's Guide to Crime Control*, by Norval Morris and Gordon Hawkins, a law professor and a criminologist respectively, suggests that we quit attempting to use criminal law as an instrument to coerce men toward virtue. The law is not suitable for such a task. Quitting our vain attempt would eliminate more than half of our six million non-traffic arrests each year.

What follows is directed toward helping those whose sense

of failure leads them to commit crimes against others, both the obvious robbers and burglars and the less obvious embezzlers and other white-collar criminals. Although the following suggestions will also aid the large group of offenders described by Morris and Hawkins, using the correctional system to help them is wasteful and unnecessary. They should be helped from failure by agencies other than the correctional system. Sometimes this occurs now. In Los Angeles, for example, a judge may direct a person convicted of heroin addiction to Synanon, which is not a correctional facility. The judge believes the person has a better chance of being rehabilitated there than being designated a criminal and sent to jail. Many programs, especially with drug users and alcoholics, use noncorrectional rehabilitation facilities such as halfway houses and Alcoholics Anonymous. We must make greater use of such programs to free our policemen from the merry-go-round of arresting, over and over, the many people who commit crimes without victims. There are more than three million such arrests per year, two million of which are for public drunkenness. Except for those who drive while they are drunk, most of those who are arrested are no danger to society, and all of them are much more failures than criminals.

To treat people whose crimes are against persons or property, we must follow the concepts of Reality Therapy, especially Principles Six and Seven that state "no excuses" and "no punishment." Because it may be difficult for many people to understand how a correctional and legal system could work that allows no excuses and uses punishment sparingly, I shall describe it. My suggestions are not radical; they are used now for those with power, influence, wealth, or a good chance for success. These people are treated differently from the young. man, Harry, whom I will use as an example. I will discuss this double standard of justice further after we consider the case of Harry, who has been arrested for armed robbery at the age of twenty-two. By that time, he has already been in several juvenile institutions for car theft, assault, and possession of narcotics. Recently he spent several months in a mental hospital after taking a large amount of LSD. His parents are divorced and he has lost touch with his father. He did badly in school and has felt failure since early in elementary school. At present, he has no one whom he can count on, whom he can call a friend. Because his mother has younger children to care for, she can visit him only occasionally and provide him with little financial or emotional support.

Under the existing system, Harry is detained before trial in county jail between thirty and two hundred days because h~ cannot make bail. Although he might be freed on his own recognizance with little fear that he would not appear for trial, we rarely grant freedom under such conditions. An interesting sidelight is that men who cannot make bail constitute more than half of those in jail. Harry spends most of his time in jail sitting around, smoking, chatting with other prisoners, and surviving as one survives in jail. He gives little thought to the future because he knows that his future will be prison or a mental hospital. Because the evidence is so strong that he did hold up a liquor store, his attorney advises him to plead not guilty by reason of diminished capacity to form a specific intent to steal. He claims that Harry was released from the mental hospital too soon and that he committed the crime under the influence of active hallucinations that told him that to rob a liquor store was a Christian act of charity. This is the kind of fairy tale that our present legal system allows. Harry's attorney has every right to represent him in any way that is legal to get him judged "not guilty." Harry is evaluated by the psychiatrist assigned by the court, who finds him nervous but with no evidence of psychosis at this time. A young psychiatrist whom Harry's attorney persuades to see Harry for no fee finds Harry still psychotic although in remission at present. He confirms Harry's vague claim of diminished capacity at the time of the crime.

After about three months in county jail, Harry's case comes to court.* Because Harry does not deny the evidence presented by the district attorney, the jury must decide which psychiatrist to believe. Under cross-examination, his psychiatrist admits he has only his clinical judgment to substantiate his claim of diminished capacity. (That is all any psychiatrist ever has.) Harry's being judged "not guilty" or "guilty" thus depends upon the reputation of his psychiatrist and his ability to present his judgment clearly and concisely to the jury. In addition to the testimony relating directly to the case, the jury also considers Harry's background of failure and the unlikelihood of his doing well if he was released. The jury cannot help taking these other considerations into account, although legally Harry is not to be held responsible for anything except the present charge. The jury finds him guilty, refusing to believe that his capacity was diminished at the time of the crime.

In California a conviction for armed robbery carries a minimum sentence of six months to life and usually five years to life in state prison. Because Harry has a long file and an unfavorable current probation report, the judge does not consider probation and sentences him to five years to life. Although the probation report did mention that Harry could use

---

* In most large cities, nine out of ten criminals like Harry plead guilty as a result of a deal offered by the district attorney. If they did not, the courts would cease to function. For his guilty plea, the offender ordinarily receives a shorter sentence than he would had he gone to trial.

psychiatric treatment, the most he will get in prison is one interview with the psychiatric social worker early in his stay and perhaps another shortly before he leaves. Assuming he gets into no serious trouble, Harry's sentence makes him eligible for parole after thirty-two months. He is released at twenty-five years of age, having served three years in prison. Despite learning some auto mechanics, he has much less confidence in his ability to work in a job with successful people than he had before his term in prison. Desperately lonely and with no one he can call a friend, he begins to look for drugs within an hour of his release. His parole officer has a caseload of 180 men like Harry and can spend almost no time with him. Unless there is a condition of essentially full employment when he is released, it will be almost impossible for him to find work. And, as an able-bodied man, he has no recourse to the welfare system.

After a few months, Harry attempts another armed robbery to support his need for drugs. Under the influence of amphetamines and reckless because he knows that he faces a long sentence in any case if he is caught, he shoots and kills the liquor store clerk who tries to resist the holdup. With nowhere to hide, he is soon apprehended. This time he does not bother with the plea of diminished capacity; he pleads guilty and accepts a life sentence. Some years ago he might have received the death penalty, but the death penalty is little used in the identity society. By pleading guilty, he can get a deal for life imprisonment, which in most states means ten to twenty-five years in prison before he is considered for parole.

What I have described happens now; it is a totally ineffective way of dealing with a serious problem. Assuming that people like Harry will continue to grow to age twenty with a failure identity and depend upon expensive drugs that lead them to commit crimes, how might we handle their cases to get a better result?

First, we must recognize that putting a man in prison is almost never correction or rehabilitation; it is punishment. Some prisons are better than others, but they are all punitive. Harry cannot become involved with responsible people in any normal way. Cut off from women, the only sexual relationship open to him is homosexual. Except for what he can create in fantasy or hostility, he is subject to a boring, routine life that does not provide the stimulation he needs to make him feel alive and useful. A quotation from the recent President's Crime Commission* emphasizes this point.

Life in many institutions is, at best, barren and futile; at worst, unspeakably brutal and degrading. To be sure, the offenders in such institutions are incapacitated from committing further crimes while serving their sentences, but the conditions in which they live are the poorest possible preparation for their successful re-entry into society and often merely reinforce in them a pattern of manipulation or destructiveness.

Let us go back to the time when Harry came into custody at age twenty-two for participating in an armed robbery and use the legal and judicial system that I believe would better serve the identity society. Under my proposed system, Harry would first have what I call a facts-only trial. If he were found guilty, he would later have a formal probation hearing before the judge. In the trial, which would usually be short, *only the facts* of the case would be presented. Psychiatric testimony, character witnesses, and attempts to reduce responsibility for the crime would not be allowed. He could be stark raving mad; he could have committed a crime to keep his children from starving; he could be the wealthiest and most influential

* Report of the President's Commission on Law Enforcement and the Administration of Justice: The Challenge of Crime in a Free Society, 1967.

man in the city; or he could have the finest character witnesses available; none would be a reason for a not-guilty judgment. Because self-defense is part of the facts, only if he had broken the law in self-defense could he be judged not guilty if he had, in fact, committed the alleged act. Thus in the trial, assuming his constitutional rights were protected, he would be judged solely on whether or not he committed the crime.

If he was found innocent, the case would of course end there. If he pleaded guilty or was found guilty, as Harry was, he could, under the procedure I suggest, ask for a formal probation hearing to present to the judge his plan for rehabilitation. If he did not want to offer a plan for rehabilitation, he could accept the existing probation system in which a probation officer presents Harry's chances in a report. The offender rarely sees this report and does not know whether the judge read it carefully or understood its full meaning. In the formal hearing Harry would himself present to the judge a detailed plan for his own rehabilitation that could be supported by evidence and testimony not allowed in the trial. Psychiatric testimony, character witnesses, and mitigating circumstances that might not occur in the future would be permitted. The prosecuting attorney's office would see the plan before the hearing. If he wished, a representative of that office could be present to make a statement rebutting Harry's plan. No cross-examination would be allowed. The judge would make his decision based on all the information presented at the hearing.

If Harry asked for, argued for, and was accepted for rehabilitation, he would not be sent to prison. Instead, he would be cared for by the probation department within his community. Rehabilitation can be defined as fulfilling the conditions that are now accepted for successfully completing probation. In most cases this means staying out of trouble and working for one to five years. In the next chapter I will suggest that, for rehabilitation to be most effective, Harry be treated in a new way through the earlier mentioned Community Involvement Center. I believe that a Community Involvement Center or some organization like it is the best way to help men like Harry if they are accepted for rehabilitation. If Harry's plea for rehabilitation was denied, he would be sent to prison for a specified term. Neither he nor anyone else would be asked to believe that prison would rehabilitate him; he would be sent there for punishment and to "protect" the community.

In prison he would have a chance to apply for rehabilitation at specified intervals. If he did not wish to apply for rehabilitation, he could accept his prison term, serve it, and be released with no obligation to do anything to rehabilitate himself. If, however, he requested rehabilitation and was paroled, it would be on the condition that he would not be released, free and clear, from his obligation until he was rehabilitated. Our present parole system is essentially what I have just described. For greater effectiveness parole as well as probation could be a function of the Community Involvement Center.

To be fair, an accused man should be told the sentence when he was judged guilty. Assume that the sentence was a year in jail. A man with a fairly firm failure identity might decide that he had no confidence in himself and in his ability to be rehabilitated and that it would be wise to serve the year in jail and then take his chances with no strings attached. Some criminals choose this course now because they do not trust probation or parole. They fear they will be sent back for a minor infraction and end up serving more time than the original sentence. Probably very few men would choose prison to possible probation, but they should be given the choice because an important part of the new correctional procedure is to give the offender as much opportunity as possible to decide his own future. Planning and commitment are important steps toward gaining a successful identity, according to Principles Four and Five of Reality Therapy. Principle Three, the value judgment, applies to the choice between attempting rehabilitation or accepting prison.

Assuming that Harry chose to present his own case for rehabilitation, he would have a reasonable period of time after the trial to develop his plan. Although he might work out his plan on his own, he would more likely be aided by counselors. Under the present system the counselors would be probation officers. Under my new suggested system of Community Involvement Centers, a court officer would assist Harry in choosing the community he would live in if he was released. Counselors from that Community Involvement Center would counsel him and would also put him in touch with anyone else who might help him formulate his plan for rehabilitation.

At this point, let me continue a previous claim that supervised release in the community is not really new. It occurs now for people who seem unlikely to repeat their crime and do not seem to be a danger to the community. Not confirmed failures and with a reasonable chance to succeed, they often have or represent power, wealth, and stature in the community. When they are found guilty of a crime—even a serious crime—they are more likely than a poor offender to be given probation. They deserve this nonpunitive chance to rehabilitate themselves because their past has been mostly successful; we need, however, more chances for those who have not been successful. The court may cooperate in a rehabilitation plan by which the person on probation may be sent to a private psychiatrist, a private mental hospital, or a well-supervised private school. Thus, a system similar to the one I suggest is in operation for some people; unfortunately for the whole community, it discriminates against the poor.

The present system also discriminates against the poor and powerless because they are almost always found guilty as charged, whereas the rich or influential are at times found not guilty when they are in fact guilty. Rationalizing that there is a reasonable doubt of guilt, the jury actually believes that the people they acquit will have a better chance to rehabilitate themselves if they have no stigma of guilt and no record. The jury is reluctant to send someone who they believe has a good chance to rehabilitate himself to prison because they know that rehabilitation will not occur there.

Unfortunately, when a person like Harry, who has a long history of failure and is thus representative of most criminals, is brought to trial, his chance is small either for acquittal (if he has committed the act) or for probation (if he is convicted). Unlike the rich, he is almost never considered seriously when he pleads diminished capacity or mental illness, pleas by which he could be found not guilty by a jury. Because most judges and most probation officers view him as a failure, he will most likely go to prison. Although he may meet a probation officer who sees a chance for rehabilitation in his bleak background and a judge who will heed his report, probation is not common.

Under my suggested system, the poor would have a better chance for probation than they do now; they would more often be treated as the rich are now. The rich would be found guilty more often than they are now because the jury would know that finding them guilty probably would not result in their going to prison. If we implement the Community Involvement Center and if we start a program of planned and supervised release with the first crime a person commits, we should be able to rehabilitate many more poor and a few more rich people than we do now.

Going back to Harry, let us say that he was given six weeks to prepare his plan. Whether he did so in jail or out on bail, he would get the help and guidance of a probation officer trained in making rehabilitation plans or the help of the Community Involvement Center counselor if such centers are implemented. He would be given information about places to live and about possible jobs. He would be guided toward meetings with his family and involved in discussion groups with other men preparing rehabilitation plans. Under the Community Involvement Center program, men who have successfully completed a rehabilitation plan would volunteer to help young men like Harry make a plan with a good chance for success. Harry would know that if his plan failed he could be sent to prison to serve the sentence that was decided on before he was accepted for rehabilitation. Although it would not be mandatory that he be sent to prison if his plan failed, the possibility would exist, especially if he was unable to suggest a reasonable revised plan. Excuses on why his plan failed would neither be asked for nor be accepted.

As I have said, the plan would require approval by the judge for Harry to be placed on probation or to become involved in a rehabilitation program through the Community Involvement Center. If his rehabilitation plan succeeded, he would be released from probation with no stigma of felony. After rehabilitation he would be asked to give time to the Community Involvement Center to help others attempting rehabilitation. Each person helped by a previously rehabilitated person would see that success is possible. Seeing that success is possible is an important part of the rehabilitation of a failure.

As an example of a plan, I shall outline one that Harry might present to a judge. Again, I am talking about the time when Harry robbed the liquor store at age twenty-two. In asking for approval of his plan, he would not want to say that he was out of his mind on drugs when he committed the robbery. Claiming mental incompetence would not be to his benefit because the judge might well think he would soon be back on drugs. He would have to show that he had a place to live with some people who cared for him. Given the Community Involvement Center, he probably could find someone through the center or he might live in a halfway house attached to the center. At the present time, under regular probation, he would have to find a family or a friend or his own family who would give him a place to live. In my experience, most probationers can find somewhere to stay, but it is rarely a good place. For Harry's rehabilitation plan to be acceptable, a good place to live would be a requirement. He would, however, have much more help in finding such a place than he does now.

It would be good for Harry to show that he had reestablished a relationship with his mother and with his younger brothers and sisters and that as part of his plan he was going to take some responsibility for his family. He would have to show that he was accepted in a training program or that he had a good plan to find a job. He might even have found a job already. If he was going into a training program, he would need a plan to find part-time work. In my experience, most men are able to find work if the choice is clear: work or jail. As a part of his plan, he might use some of his pay to repay his robbery victim in part. If repayment was part of the plan, the victim might testify on Harry's behalf. This occasionally occurs today and would be more common if more victims were repaid.

To help make his plan acceptable to a judge, a chronic failure like Harry can include some voluntary service to the community. Many of our community resources, such as parks, beaches, and hospitals, need volunteer workers. Our schools need night watchmen to prevent vandalism. Harry could volunteer to work through his Community Involvement Center. At present, a probationer who wishes to do volunteer work is usually unacceptable because of his record. If such work were available and supervised as part of the Community Involvement Center program, men like Harry could be used. His plan would also show how he planned to use some of his spare time. For example, he might join a bowling league.

To emphasize the point that I have made repeatedly—that prison is not rehabilitation—I shall quote a letter printed in the Los Angeles *Times* in the spring of 1971. The letter was written by John Severnson Watson, editor of the San Quentin *News*, the newspaper of San Quentin (California) Prison. As a preface to the letter, he says:

Let me clarify a few points: 1) I'm the author of the article, 2) I'm a "lifer," 3) I've got no one but myself to blame for being here.

However, none of the above comments changes the accurate point of view expressed. No one who has ever done "time" can dispute the accuracy of the statements made on rehabilitation.

Nothing succeeds like failure. Disbelievers of that comment can check the size of the payroll for the California Department of Corrections.

In the letter itself, Mr. Watson says:

Rehabilitation is . . . being sentenced to state prison for treatment and punishment . . . and finding out there is little if any of the former and a lot of the latter.

Rehabilitation is . . . going before disciplinary court with no prior infractions and being told you're conwise. Or going to the same committee with half a dozen minor violations over a two year period (e.g., a pound of butter found in your cell with five peanut butter priors) and being told you're an obvious nonconforming and rebellious individual.

Rehabilitation is . . . living, eating, sleeping and working with the dregs of society and yet being expected to improve your outlook on life and solve your hangups.

Rehabilitation is . . . being sentenced to the Adjustment Center, because of past disciplinary infractions, to a "program." There is no program but isolation. There is no adjustment except for the worse.

Rehabilitation is . . . seeing your enemies getting parole dates and swallowing hard. It's seeing your best (and maybe only) friend get a "date" and having mixed emotions . . . you're glad for him . . . and sad for yourself because you know you're really going to miss the guy.

Rehabilitation is . . . trying to control the self-contempt for being in the prison environment . . . and losing the battle.

Rehabilitation is . . . seeing the daily incompetence and inefficiency of some of the free people working here . . . the same people who are supposed to be setting the correct example for you on the road to being a good citizen.

Rehabilitation is . . . having a prison official take a sincere interest in you and your future . . . and wondering if this one plus will offset the dozen negative factors in your everyday life.

Rehabilitation is . . . having the judge, the jury and the professional staff at the Guidance Center strongly recommend psychiatric treatment during your incarceration . . . and seeing the head shrinker once a year for 30 minutes.

Rehabilitation is . . . being paroled, reporting to the parole officer promptly, and being told at the start of the conversation that if you make one false move you're on your way back to prison.

If more people were allowed to attempt rehabilitation under the present system, more probation and parole officers would be needed. In direct financial terms, they are a good expenditure for the state because probation or parole costs less than 10 percent of the cost of prisons. California recently completed two large juvenile reformatories that will not be opened because they are not yet needed. A state-subsidized probation program has been so successful that for the first time in twenty years there is no need for more juvenile prisons. Present probation, even with overworked probation officers, is usually better than 60 percent successful. The case overload leads to many failures in probation, however, because it is difficult for the probationer to get involved with his officer. Reducing caseloads will make probation more effective and save even more money. To back my claim of the value of treating the criminal in the community, let me again quote from the President's Crime Commission:

> The correctional strategy that presently seems to hold the greatest promise, based on social science theory and limited research, is that of reintegrating the offender into the community. It . . . means avoiding as much as possible the isolating and labeling effects of commitment to an institution. There is little doubt that the goals of reintegration are furthered much more readily by working with an offender in the community than by incarcerating him.

To see how these suggestions would work with a different kind of offender, consider a bank clerk or a bank officer who has embezzled a large sum of money. A far more common crime than most people suspect, embezzlement causes much greater monetary loss than robberies and burglaries cost together.

In the trial, there would be no mitigating circumstances admitted as evidence, no character witnesses, and no lesser plea. The accused man would be found guilty of grand theft. As Harry had done, he would apply for rehabilitation and present his plan. Despite a successful skill and a good plan, he might still be sentenced to prison because embezzlement is a crime that is tempting to many people who feel failure and who want more money than they have. Although putting the banker in jail is not beneficial to him, it does show the community that something was done, and it might be a deterrent to those tempted to try embezzling. Bankers are rarely sent to jail; if more were, even for a short term, the amount of embezzlement would be reduced. If knowing that other people have been sent to prison is a deterrent to anyone, it is a deterrent to people who have experienced some financial success but who are dissatisfied because they want more.

Sometimes a man is insane at the time he commits a crime. Under my suggested procedures, he would be found guilty. If he was now sane, as is often the case, he could prepare his own request for rehabilitation. If he was still insane, his attorney or even the prosecuting attorney might ask for rehabilitation because the man could not prepare the plan himself. The rehabilitation plan would consist primarily of receiving psychiatric treatment. Treatment would be available in a specialized facility or in a community facility such as I describe in the next chapter. The man would not be sent to prison, because almost no psychiatric treatment is available there; there are only 50 full-time psychiatrists for the 400,000 prison inmates in the United States. The public would be assured that he would get the treatment he needs rather than, as sometimes occurs now, his being found not guilty by reason of insanity. Lawyers often plead that the accused person was insane at the time of the crime but that he is now sane. Some people who have committed crimes are thus found not guilty and freed. Most, however, go to a state hospital for a period of time to make sure they are sane; if they are, they are then released.

To illustrate the last point, let me quote a portion of an article from the Los Angeles *Times,* January 19, 1971, about the trial at Fort Benning, Georgia, of Lieutenant William Calley, who was accused of murdering, 102 villagers at My Lai:

Judge Kennedy agreed the sanity board would consist of three Army psychiatrists who served in Vietnam and whose qualifications are endorsed by the American Psychiatric Association. Under Army regulations, it must examine Calley and decide whether, at the time he is alleged to have gunned down women, children and old men, he was "so far free from mental defects, disease or derangement as to be able . . . to distinguish right from wrong . . . [and] adhere to the right."

The board's report will go to Judge Kennedy, with whatever Calley told of his actions at My Lai kept away from the prosecution lest it unfairly enhance its case. If the board finds Calley was incapable at the time of doing right, Kennedy could drop the case, and Calley would be free. The Army sends mentally disturbed soldiers to its hospital at Valley Forge, Pa., but it is already overcrowded. Chances are, Calley would simply walk off into civilian life.

If Calley is found to have been responsible for choosing the right, as well as knowing it from wrong, the trial would go on in a battle of psychiatrists—Calley's versus the sanity board—and the jury would consider that testimony with all the rest. Its impact might never be known, since jurors need not say what persuaded them.

I believe the procedure described in the article is wrong. It attempts to use psychiatry incorrectly. It is not possible for a psychiatrist (or anyone else, for that matter) to determine whether or not a man was incapable of knowing what he was doing or, even further, whether he could distinguish right from wrong. The best that a psychiatrist can do is to state that in his opinion the present mental condition of the offender is such that he has a chance for successful rehabilitation and that psychiatric treatment would increase the likelihood of success. Almost all other use of psychiatry in both criminal and civil trials usually becomes little more than a personality and prestige contest between psychiatrists cast in adversary roles. Rules for insanity such as McNaughten (the accused was incapable of distinguishing that what he did was wrong) and Durham (the crime of the accused was a product of his mental illness) are now used to avoid guilt by claiming insanity. Such pleas would not be allowed in my suggested system of a facts-only trial and a formal probation hearing. Guilt would be determined by behavior. The only question asked would be whether or not the accused committed the crime. If he was found guilty, the only question to be resolved is whether or not he is a good candidate for rehabilitation.

I believe that with extremely rare exceptions, usually produced by drugs or a toxic disease, people always know what they are doing when they commit an act, criminal or not, that involves others. Never have I personally encountered a person who had done anything involving others under the influence of drugs or under the influence of emotional instability who did not know what he was doing at the time he was doing it. I discount almost all of the arguments that criminal behavior should be excused on the basis of insanity, the influence of drugs, or other psychological circumstances. Even the stress of poverty, revenge, or jealousy, which may lead to crime and then be used to excuse or partially excuse the crime, is more valid as evidence for rehabilitation, assuming the situation now has changed for the better, than as evidence for a person's being found not guilty. I believe that a person can become so involved with himself that he does not care what he does; in this condition, he may commit a crime. Lack of caring, however, would not be a good argument at the rehabilitation hearing because a man who was so detached and so noncaring that he committed a serious crime would not be a good candidate for rehabilitation. In fact, the shoe would be on the other foot; it would be more likely that the prosecution would state that his insanity was evidence that he should be sent to a competent, closed mental hospital rather than to the community. The defense would tend to downplay his insanity to bolster his claim that he is ready for community rehabilitation. When a man who does not care what he is doing and tries to deny reality is sent to prison, the prison authorities would decide whether the prison has a good program for him or whether he should be sent to a mental hospital.

Even in sensational trials such as those of Jack Ruby and Sirhan Sirhan, the accused would be treated more fairly using the system I have suggested than he is now. Guilt would be established on the facts. Conflicting psychiatric testimony and political considerations would be reserved for the probation hearing; they would be used much less than they are now because many of these arguments would make a judge less likely to agree to an attempt at rehabilitation than he would otherwise. It is neither rehabilitative for the criminal nor protective to society to clear a man of murder by reason of insanity as we sometimes do now.

As I have said, only about 15 percent of the people in prison need to be there because they are dangerous to society. Perhaps a few of the remaining 85 percent serve as an example to others to deter crime, but none receives benefit from his punishment. There is some evidence that, partly by their past record and partly by their present behavior, we can identify the dangerous 15 percent. These men would be denied release to the community and sent to prison as they are now. Whatever danger we may undergo when we fail to identify a dangerous man would more than be balanced by the others rehabilitated without prison who might have become dangerous after a term in prison.

We may persist in incarceration of persons who do not need institutional control. We can take a minor property offender and help him to develop into a more serious offender by unnecessary and long incarceration as surely as if we conducted vocational training in hate, violence, selfishness, abnormal sex relations, and criminal techniques.*

The wide publicity given anyone who commits a serious crime while on probation or parole has served to continue the fear in the minds of many that it is not safe to let criminals leave prison. We need a good system of public relations for prisoners who succeed and an understanding of the danger of the despondent failures who are eventually released after many years of punishment with, in their minds, little or no choice other than to prey on the community.

If the plan emphasizing rehabilitation that I have described were in effect, prison population would drastically drop. Prison programs could be better than they are in the present overcrowded prisons. Few men will learn to be successful in prison, however, no matter how much the prisons are improved.

The suggested procedures in this chapter could be adopted by a city, county, or federal court on a trial basis. There is no reason to believe that what we are doing now is better; there are many valid reasons to believe it is far worse.

* California Youth and Adult Corrections Agency: "The Organization of State Correctional Services in the Control and Treatment of Crime and Delinquency," 1967.

Chapter Ten

The Community
Involvement Center

Even those people who do not accept the idea of the identity society will probably agree that the social institutions of the survival society are largely ineffective. I did not discuss an effective prison in the previous chapter because I do not believe that such a prison is possible. Neither do I believe that our welfare system will work to help anyone become successful; greatly in need of personal involvement, welfare clients are given only bare physical subsistence. The treatment of alcoholics, drug addicts, school failures, dropouts, mental patients, and chronically injured and disabled people is rarely effective. The present methods of treatment do not work because, except for a few organizations such as Alcoholics Anonymous and Synanon, they do not recognize the need for involvement; they fail because they perpetuate loneliness and failure. We need institutions that serve the human need for involvement, which in the identity society is no longer being suppressed. In this chapter I suggest and will describe briefly such an institution, the Community Involvement Center. The concept of the center is that each community would have its own organization to help its failing people, no matter what symptoms they exhibit.

We can estimate the number of people the center would serve by adding the number of people in the community on probation, on parole, or in custody; those in chronic hospitals or being treated for a chronic failure such as drug addiction or alcoholism; and those on welfare or unemployed when jobs for them are available. Because the Community Involvement Center should be small enough to offer its clients personal, interested, involved service, I suggest that it serve no more than three hundred people. In communities with many failures, the centers would be closely spaced. Where there were fewer failing people, the centers would be farther apart. In no case would a person need to travel far to reach a Community Involvement Center. If people must travel far, those who need the services of the center most will not make the effort. Offices and meeting rooms of various sizes are needed in the center. Existing buildings might be used or new buildings might be built.

To explain the operation of the Community Involvement Center, I will continue the case of Harry from the previous chapter. If Harry was allowed to attempt rehabilitation instead of being sent to prison, the plan he presented to the court would have been worked out with the aid of personnel from a Community Involvement Center. If he was in jail, someone from the center would come there; if he was out on bail, he would go to the center. After Harry's plan for rehabilitation had been accepted by the judge, he would report to the center. There he would be assigned to a professional counselor who would help him get situated where he had arranged to live and perhaps obtain a small loan from the center to help him subsist until he got his first paycheck. Proposals to grant a long-term prisoner a small monthly subsidy to help him get started are now before the California legislature.

The usual caseload for Harry's professional counselor would be thirty-five to forty persons. In this group at any time about three, close to completing their plan, would volunteer to help people like Harry. They would continue as long as needed for their charge to complete his plan and to show he was rehabilitated. Although some would not wish to help, others would enjoy doing so. Most people welcome the warmth and success they gain by helping someone who they know needs their help. Their volunteer work would be as helpful to them in sustaining their success as it would be to Harry in getting his started. Continuing for many years by taking on new cases as present ones terminate, they would assure an adequate supply of volunteers. One of these men or women would be assigned to Harry as his personal counselor on a one-to-one or at most a two-to-one basis. He would thus have both the professional counselor employed by the center, who would see him by appointment or sometimes in emergencies, and the voluntary counselor, who would usually be available when he needed help or companionship. Having gone through rehabilitation successfully himself, the volunteer would understand it well and would be able to give Harry the kind of "savvy" aid possible only from someone with firsthand experience. My suggestions for volunteer help have good precedent; Alcoholics Anonymous and similar organizations are based on this kind of assistance.

A key part of the center program would be to involve Harry in a Reality Therapy discussion group of perhaps ten to twenty men and women. Composed not only of criminals in varying stages of rehabilitation but also of others with a failure identity, the groups would follow the principles of Reality Therapy or of a therapy with similar concerns for involvement and responsibility. Members of the group would become involved with one another, bring out what each person was doing, ask for value judgments, make plans, and get commitments. Although each member of the group would know that many people cared about him, he would have no excuse for not doing what he committed himself to do. The group would provide the involvement that Harry desperately needs. People who had completed rehabilitation and criminals who had been discharged from probationary status would be invited to stay with the group both to help themselves further and to help people like Harry get started.

The professional counselor and especially the volunteer would talk to Harry's family and to his employer as it was needed. They would also assist Harry to get involved in the community assistance plan discussed in the previous chapter. Each center would develop its own plan. For example, if a park was near Harry's Community Involvement Center, he and others might assist the park professionals run the various programs at the park as well as help keep the area clean. The center might get permission from the owners of vacant land nearby to develop mini-parks, an idea now working successfully in some cities. Civic volunteer work by men and women on probation would be part of the continuous rehabilitation program of the Community Involvement Center.

As Harry progressed through the center, as he became more involved, and as he discovered the strength and the warmth of having a place to go where people cared about him and helped him gain success, he would continually satisfy the two requirements for a successful identity: love and worth. Following Reality Therapy, he would be involved and he would be working on a plan to gain success. The Community Involvement Center is a practical application of Reality Therapy.

In addition to Harry, who was a criminal, the center would serve people in the neighborhood who at the present time would be sent to a mental hospital or a mental hygiene clinic. Most mental hospitals today are reducing their patient load through community psychiatric clinics. Patients do not stay long in the hospital when there is a good clinic in the community to send them to for further treatment. There will always be some people who fail who chose to become involved with psychological symptoms; if we treat them quickly and close to home through a neighborhood center always open to their needs, we will not need large mental hospitals. Instead of mental hospitals, a psychiatric unit in a neighborhood hospital working closely with the patient's Community Involvement Center will be satisfactory.

Mental patients need intensive, one-to-one, volunteer help as well as a continuing group that meets at least twice a week. Most people served by the center would get to know one another; they should be welcome daily if they wish to attend a group other than their own. The volunteers would be those who had become successful and given up their psychological symptoms or others in the center who wanted to help and had the skill. Professionals are often so impressed with crazy symptoms that they do not realize that people need involvement and a good plan to do some worthwhile work, rather than the "recognition" for their craziness that they too often get under traditional psychotherapy. Workers from the center would also counsel members of the patient's family. They could be guided toward getting more involved with him to prevent reinvolvement with himself and a relapse into his previous symptoms.

Private agencies and private practitioners would need a reputation for effectiveness to attract clients in competition with the Community Involvement Centers. Certainly, effective organizations such as Alcoholics Anonymous and Synanon would continue. Anyone who sought help privately would also be welcome for more help at his center, and private practitioners would be encouraged to use the center to supplement their necessarily brief hours of treatment.

People with chronic physical ailments, many of which serve as a way to become involved with oneself as a failure, could be helped to learn to succeed despite their handicap. As I have already recommended for both probationers attempting rehabilitation and mentally disturbed people, they should be included in the therapy groups and aided by a personal volunteer. The center program for chronically disabled people, most of whom are now handled in vocational rehabilitation programs, would include very little time in which their present or past symptoms or treatment was discussed. The time and effort would be devoted to getting them to recognize their potential for successful efforts despite their handicap. Being mixed with others in a therapy group and in other center programs would help them. In most hospitals they are now usually segregated in wards for the chronically disabled, where their forced association with others like themselves usually causes them to reinforce each other's failure.

Limited medical care should be available at each center. There are many medical procedures that do not require great expertise but now take hours of travel and long waits in county hospitals, often just to see a nurse or technician. Patients would spend much less time in travel and waiting if these procedures were performed in the Community Involvement Center. The medical delivery system described by Dr. Sidney

Garfield and briefly mentioned in Chapter Three would mesh perfectly into the Community Involvement Center. The primary health personnel would be medical corpsmen who would see everyone initially, treat what they are trained to treat, and refer those patients who needed the care of a physician. The corpsmen would be similar to those who serve so effectively in our armed forces. A training program could be created for corpsmen planning to work in Community Involvement Centers. People being rehabilitated through the center, like Harry, might volunteer to help the center corpsmen. They might thereby gain the motivation to take the corpsmen training themselves.

The center might also serve as the welfare agency for those in its community, assuming a welfare program was in effect with the same goals as the center's. That is, it would be a program in which people would get involved in groups, make plans to help themselves, and be helped by those who had used plans made through the center to get off welfare. Such a program would eliminate some of the serious flaws of the present system, which in addition to large size, central administration, and impersonal treatment of clients, offers little counseling and no group involvement.

Most of the programs suggested for the Community Involvement Center—criminal rehabilitation, mental hygiene, health screening, and the administration of welfare—exist now in a variety of agencies and institutions. They are in operation in the armed forces, through private agencies, through free clinics, and through neighborhood halfway houses. The Community Involvement Center would integrate these services and place them within reach of those who need them. Each center would have an advisory board drawn from people of the community, including those the center serves.

The center could also serve as a job placement agency for local employers who need a nonskilled or temporary employee. Harry, for example, might be placed in a job through the center. Local employers might be persuaded to contact the center when they have skilled or permanent jobs available. Because work is such an important part of rehabilitation, a computer could tie a group of centers together to refer the people the center serves to jobs in other parts of the city. Employment counseling would include interviewing the employer after a man was working to see how he was doing. Through this follow-up, the center might guide him toward training that would help him perform better.

Some people need help on a live-in basis. Alcoholics, for example, need someone available all the time to talk to when they feel lonely; if they have no one, they drink. The center or a group of centers should provide a house for people to live where they could get the necessary counseling from professionals and from volunteers drawn from the ranks of the rehabilitated who would staff the house continuously. The cost could be kept low by having the residents do some of the work. Taking some responsibility for housekeeping is a good prelude to work for people with psychological symptoms who have not worked for a long time. In addition, several centers together could sponsor housing without resident counselors. Men and women could live cooperatively, sharing the work and expenses. Living alone is bad; it is among the most painful of all experiences. The center should urge its clients not to do so.

Staffing the center and training the staff would not be difficult. We have many social workers, probation and parole officers, employment counselors, and vocational rehabilitation counselors who are doing much of what I describe in this chapter. There are also a few community psychiatrists and psychologists available now who would work well in a Community Involvement Center. Pilot centers could be staffed easily to both develop and test the center idea.

If many centers are planned and established, colleges will create programs geared to their work. The centers would then serve as fieldwork placement agencies. Training both in individual counseling and in leading groups would be included. Students would participate in the center from the start of their training; the internship would be continuous and, as their training increased, they would be given more responsibility. Working directly under the supervision of the center professionals, the students would help all of the people served by the center. A student might start the training after two years of college and complete it in three more years; he would then receive his degree, perhaps a bachelor's degree in community center counseling.

I will not at this time attempt to describe further the detailed operation of a Community Involvement Center. What I have described is within the scope of our existing knowledge, but it has not yet been put together systematically. Establishing a few pilot centers is feasible and should be done now.

Conclusion

In this book I have tried to describe our new identity society and to suggest some ways to live successfully in it. As I continue to work and to think about what needs to be done, I realize that our real chance to succeed in this new society will depend on our ability to cooperate intelligently and become involved with one another for our common good. We have no good precedent for many people getting together and working for change without coercive force. We have grown to depend on forceful change; when we have had wise and humane leaders it has worked fairly well. Less and less willing to be coerced, we no longer listen to or follow leaders with the fear or the long-term devotion, usually both, with which we followed them in the past. We are afraid that we will not be able to build and use relationships we realize we now need but for which we have no precedent. Although we may say that we are looking for a leader to guide us, we will not follow any leader as we did in the past because we soon begin to question his leadership; we refuse to surrender part of our newly won identity. We must get together and plan among ourselves for a better world, to try to follow as a guide the little footpath of involvement and cooperation that has almost disappeared because it has been little used and poorly tended for the 10,000 survival society years. In the past twenty-five years there have been signs that we are learning to use it again. It is my hope that this book will alert us to repair and enlarge this path, and to encourage everyone we can to join with us in its use.

Appendix

Shortly after starting this book in the spring of 1969, I realized that my attempts to trace man's behavior back four million years had led me deep into speculative anthropology. For assistance I consulted Professor Burton Siskin, chairman of the Department of Anthropology, Los Angeles Valley College. With his help, I was able to explain my main ideas, especially the concept of the primitive identity society, in a way consistent with current anthropological knowledge. To back our position, Professor Siskin makes the following brief statement:

Anyone who describes what our earliest ancestors felt or thought must speculate. As anthropological consultant I made use of two sources of information about early man. First, some remains of early man exist, including his tools, his living sites. and his own bones. Second, many simple hunting societies that may well be like those of early man have survived until the present century. Groups such as the Pygmies of the Ituri Forest of the Congo and the Bushmen of the Kalahari Desert of Southwest Africa have been studied extensively.

The clues left by our ancestors show that an important change took place about 500,000 years ago with the discovery of fire. Before this time man led a meager existence. With a small brain and rudimentary tools, his hunting was apparently confined to small game. Living on the savannas of Africa, he was in danger of attack from various large predators. His camp sites contain only the bones of small animals and extremely crude all-purpose cutting tools.

By the time man developed fire, his brain had grown to a size approaching that of modern man and his tool kit had become diversified. Using fire to drive the animals, man became a big game hunter. The bones found in his hunting camps are mostly those of large animals, especially elephants. It is likely that the largest, most powerful animal was singled out for the hunt to demonstrate the bravery of the hunters. When men try to show they are brave, they are seeking an identity as well as a meal.

In recent hunting societies that we have studied, the sharing of food is usually institutionalized so that an adult male has little economic need to hunt. Social pressure, however, requires that he hunt to maintain his identity as a hunter. Monographs such as the Marshalls' studies of the Kalahari Bushmen and Colin Turnbull's study of the Ituri Forest Pygmies give good examples of this kind of pressure.

Because this book is not about anthropology, I have not presented a detailed defense of the position we take. Professor Siskin would welcome a scholarly inquiry or challenge from readers who wish more evidence or who question the conclusions.

As recognizable human beings, we have been living on earth for about four million years. During this time we went through many evolutionary changes, arriving at our present physical structure about 50,000 years ago. Although our physical structure has been fixed for 50,000 years and has been essentially human for millions of years, our behavior has varied widely over this time. Variable as it was and still is, all that we do is governed by two factors: our total nervous system and our conscious mind. Our nervous system urges us to protect ourselves and, when we are safe, to enjoy ourselves. Our mind must choose what seems best from the possibilities that we recognize are open to us. When our mind and our nervous system are in harmony, we feel good; when they conflict, as they often do, we suffer. For example, although suffering intense fear, most soldiers obey orders and go into battle, thus choosing to override their nervous system, which sends a constant stream of messages to their conscious mind urging them to change their behavior and run.

We must learn to satisfy, to the extent we can, what our nervous system urges, and at the same time, we must learn to choose the best options available in our new society. I call this new society the *civilized identity society;* later I will often refer to it as the new society or the identity society. The civilized identity society is hardly twenty years old, but in this short time we have changed our behavior drastically and we are still enmeshed in rapid change. To put this new behavior into perspective, we must compare what we do now in the new civilized identity society with the better understood behavior of the previous society, the *survival society.* This previous society ended rather abruptly for about half a billion people in the Western world around the year 1950. Many of us do not realize this change has taken place, that in the midst of our lives, a 10,000-year-old society has ended and a new society begun.

To understand both man today in the civilized identity society and man prior to 1950 in the survival society, we must go back four million years and examine man as he evolved slowly through two earlier, primitive societies: the *primitive survival society,* which existed for three and a half million years, and the *primitive identity society,* which existed for half a million years, ending as civilization began about 10,000 years ago. The primitive survival society and the primitive identity society have counterparts in the survival society and the civilized identity society. For ready reference, the four societies, their order, the time of their existence, and their main motivation are summarized in Table 1.

During the three and a half million years of the earliest society, the *primitive survival society,* puny as we were, we survived a rigorous, often hostile environment because we

Table 1

THE FOUR SOCIETIES OF MAN

SOCIETY	BEGAN	ENDED	MAIN MOTIVATION
Primitive Survival	4,000,000 years ago	500,000 years ago	Intelligent cooperation
Primitive Identity	500,000 years ago	10,000 years ago	Involvement
Survival	10,000 years ago	A.D. 1950 (approx.)	Power
Civilized Identity	A.D. 1950 to ?		Involvement and cooperation

cooperated intelligently with one another. For millions of years people cooperated to defend themselves against predatory animals, to kill for food, to raise their helpless young, and to help each other in a thousand intelligent ways to overcome their individual weaknesses. When they did not cooperate, they suffered; sometimes they died. During this time, the need for intelligent cooperation became built into our nervous system by the normal evolutionary process of natural selection. It is not surprising that man started with an innate tendency for cooperation, considering the cooperative behavior seen today in many of man's primitive relations.

Because we base most of our knowledge about man and his behavior on the past few thousand years, not upon the millions of years of our evolution, the ancient neurological need for intelligent cooperation is poorly understood. We do not recognize how much this need affects us because for one hundred centuries, the brief time of civilization, we have denied its urges. The stresses and strains during the 10,000 years of the civilized survival society have forced our minds to choose survival behavior that conflicts with the cooperative behavior which became a part of our nervous system during the two primitive societies. In the survival society most men learned to ignore the suffering and deprivation that existed all around them. Because hostile, antagonistic behavior which, in turn, provoked similar defensive behavior has been so much a part of our civilized history, it is easy to see how scholars of man have erroneously concluded that aggression and antagonism, not cooperation, are innate human qualities. The reasons for man's hostile behavior are described later in a discussion of the survival society. To succeed in the post-1950 identity society, we must base our knowledge of man not upon the learned behavior of 10,000 years—antagonism and hostility—but upon the innate behavior of four million years—cooperation and friendly competition.

As early man cooperated successfully, he was able to enjoy increasing periods of rest and freedom from stress. During these leisure times, he learned to enjoy the company of his fellow man, to be motivated to cooperate not just for survival but also for pleasure. As this pleasure occurred more and more frequently over the millions of years that man slowly gained competence to overcome surrounding dangers, the ancient need for intelligent cooperation evolved into a sister need, *the need for involvement, the need for man to be with his fellow man.* About 500,000 years ago, man so successfully overcame the dangers to life that little time was needed for working cooperatively to survive; as a result he was able to spend most of his time enjoying the society of other men. At this time, the need for involvement became fixed in our nervous system. From then until now, this innate need urges us to be with one another and to develop a wide variety of ways to enjoy one another's company.

Because the need for involvement is built into our nervous system, when we are alone—unless by choice—we feel pain. Our nervous system uses pain to tell us to get involved with someone. We may understand that it is safe to be alone, that we are cared for and loved, that being alone is temporary; yet, when we are alone, we feel some discomfort because our need for involvement is unsatisfied. Under most circumstances during the past 500,000 years, it has been impossible to be alone without feeling the same pain that we felt previously when we failed to cooperate intelligently. The pain is perhaps less acute and less easy to relate to a cause than is the pain of failure to cooperate for survival; nevertheless, when we are alone or lonely, we hurt in various ways. Even when we are with others, if they provide no stimulation and therefore little involvement, we will feel at least the minimum pain of boredom. To live successfully in our present society, we must recognize that the need for stimulating social and intellectual involvement is a part of us, that it evolved from a need that kept us alive, and that it warns us to seek each other's company through the same urgent nervous paths that its ancient predecessor used. Like it or not, we need each other.

It is a common belief that life became easier with the advent of civilization, the recorded history of settled, agricultural, property-owning societies during the past 5,000 to 10,000 years. Commonly held as is this belief, there is little evidence that it is true. In fact, there is good evidence that the lives of two-thirds of the people in the world today and the lives of almost all people who lived during the 10,000 years of the *survival society* are, and were, much less satisfactory from the standpoint of ease and human satisfaction than were the lives of men who lived half a million years before in the *primitive identity society*.

Both civilized survival man and primitive survival man were hard pressed to survive the stresses of their environment. Both groups worked to survive, but with one major difference. Primitive survival man struggled against a hostile, natural environment not of his own making; *civilized survival man struggled and struggles against a hostile environment almost all of his own making.* Primitive survival man suffered from lack of food, lack of shelter, lack of ability to make tools and materials to survive, but he got along with his fellow man. Civilized survival man has demonstrated an outstanding ability to utilize the resources of his environment to his own advantage. He has not, however, demonstrated except for brief periods an ability to get along with his fellow man.

The *primitive identity society*, a 500,000-year period during which men lived enjoyably together, intervened between the *primitive survival society* and the *survival society*. We have some evidence that primitive identity man lived peacefully with his fellows in a fairly abundant, nonstressful environment. Having learned to hunt efficiently and gather prudently, he gained the leisure time necessary to develop small, sometimes complex societies. Although conflict existed in the life of primitive identity man, it resembled neither the environmental struggle of primitive survival man nor the vicious fratricide of civilized survival man.

During this time of ease, men were able to become deeply involved with one another; there was time to think, to have fun and, for those who were unsuccessful in becoming involved, to learn the pain of loneliness. For half a million years man lived in a society in which *his human needs and human gratification—his identity—were his major concern.* The primitive identity society gradually replaced the primitive survival society of the previous three and a half million years during which man worked and cooperated just to survive—activity constant enough to preclude the possibility of extensive enjoyment of one's own humanity.

Man developed and enjoyed many of the innate pleasures possible through his nervous system at this time. Easily able to satisfy his physiological needs, he had ample time to develop his culture and his relationships with his fellow man. He formulated many complex kinship systems, rituals, ceremonies, dances, and religious beliefs to further personal identity. Man learned to use his brain and his body for mutual enjoyment and satisfaction. The pleasure of sex was particularly prized. In our new civilized identity society, the open recognition of sex as an important human pleasure has again become accepted, an occurrence discussed further in Chapter Eight.

If there were many children in the primitive identity society, there was room to spread out; so few people existed that children could leave, find new territory, and quickly form a nonstressful but usually complex society as had their parents and grandparents. During this time, when people could relax and live easily, it is likely that magic, religion, art, and music developed. Power and property were not important.

Wars or conflicts between groups were identity wars fought for personal status rather than power. Wars were neither organized nor lengthy; people did not systematically kill or enslave each other, nor did they prey wantonly upon one another. There was no need to do so. Even cannibals ate the flesh of human victims to obtain for themselves the spirit—in a sense the identity—of the person eaten rather than to survive.

One recent and one present example of primitive identity

societies are the Cheyenne Indians of the Great Plains and the Kung Bushmen of the Kalahari Desert in southern Africa. The Cheyenne were a typical Plains Indian society. The problem of survival was solved by an annual cooperative buffalo hunt in which thousands of buffaloes were killed. Some aspects of the hunt itself make more sense in terms of identity than survival. For example, although the hunt's proceeds were divided evenly among the tribe's families, each young warrior strove to kill as many buffalo as he could, not to give his family more food but to enhance his social standing in the tribe. Warfare, which occupied much of the year, was embellished with displays of bravery that did little to ensure victory: bravery became an end in itself. Thus prestige drives overrode the more limited military requirements, making war a game rather than a quest for power or property.

The Kung Bushmen, who have no single source of food equal to the buffalo, hunt continually during most of the year. About 80 percent of their food is supplied by the women who gather edible plants and nuts, and only 20 percent is gained by hunting. Because most game animals are divided equally among the members of the tribe, the hunter receives no larger share than any other male. Still, because of great social pressure, the male spends most of his time hunting, even though it has little to do with increasing his chance of survival. He would be better off gathering, if survival were primary.

These two societies follow the general pattern of what was once a large number of primitive identity cultures. Population tended to be small and put little pressure on available food resources. Because little time was needed to deal with problems of survival, personal activities such as hunting and, in the case of the Cheyenne, warfare became elaborate means to stress individual accomplishment and prestige.

People in these societies were role-oriented; they cared about their individual identity, their own personal pleasure, and their involvement with others. By creating intellectual activities to support their involvement and personal identity, such as elaborate rituals of magic and religion, they impressed themselves and others with their status, worth, and personal accomplishments—their role as individuals and as a society. As time for personal involvement increased, they developed more and more complex ways to enhance and maintain their role or identity. Compared with the way most people live today, it was a good time to be alive.

During a period of several thousand years, primitive identity societies ended in many parts of the world when easily obtainable game became scarce. Population increased until man outstripped the environment's capacity to furnish him abundant food. The discovery of agriculture, an important means of survival, caused land to become valuable. To ensure access to land man began to prey upon his fellows. Conflict became the rule, not the exception, as man moved into the survival society. A few societies, such as the Hopi Indians of Arizona, retained identity society characteristics despite population expansion and movement into organized farming communities. These societies, however, often living in out-of-the-way, hard-to-farm places, were infrequent and most have not survived the twentieth century.

Lack of easily obtainable game explains why some primitive identity societies ended, but it cannot explain the rapid and almost complete destruction of all primitive identity societies by the twentieth century. Their destruction was sealed when early civilized men learned to use the tools and practices of war to expand their territory and resources at the expense of weaker neighbors. Once the idea of conquest became common, aggressive men spread rapidly over the world in search of easy riches. To steal land and resources, they overpowered, enslaved, or destroyed men who posed no danger to them. Because of their innate need for involvement, the conquerors probably had brief guilt pangs that were, however, easily overcome by a multitude of moral excuses, all of which were rationalizations of the claim that the stolen resources were necessary for their own survival. Our American Indians are a classic example of primitive identity societies destroyed by survival societies.

The survival society was a goal-oriented society, a society in which men became mutually involved to protect themselves and to overcome weaker, less organized, less belligerent fellows. To survive, men relinquished their individuality and became subservient to the group. Work became necessary, and to ensure their own survival, strong men forced or persuaded others to labor for them. The control by one man of other men characterized the society. Most men lost their pleasure-dominated role orientation and, struggling to survive, reverted to a pain-dominated goal orientation.

Men were able to concern themselves with a role only after ensuring their security. In the survival society concern with role was possible for few men. Even for these few the role was not a freely chosen role independent of goal such as characterized the primitive identity society but a limited, specialized, dependent role related to a survival or security goal; for example, a soldier fought, a politician led, a cleric prayed. Most men struggled continually to survive. They had no role or identity—independent or dependent. Only during frequent wars were they able to gain even the severely restricted role of the expendable soldier. Because this dangerous role was attractive to men with no identity, there was rarely a shortage of soldiers.

In any survival society some men were able to gain an independent role and concern themselves primarily with the pleasure of involvement with those like themselves. Others, who aspired to be like them, saw these men as a key to their own independence. A few men who attained an independent role tried to help the many men who had little chance for a life beyond bare survival. These men are recorded in history as the great humanitarians. They were always few, however frequently history mentions them, and much as they tried, their effect was limited. Lincoln freed the slaves, but he could do little to improve the life of black Americans beyond bare survival.

Civilization forced most men to suppress, delay, or alter their need for involvement. Because this need was intrinsic, its suppression was painful. But if men did not suppress it, if they attempted to get involved with their enemies, they did not survive. The history of America reveals many incidents in which the Indians attempted friendship and were then quickly betrayed and slaughtered. As men suppressed their need for involvement to survive, goal effectively replaced role.

In survival societies most people have no identity and live in constant frustration because their need for involvement is unfulfilled. Even today most people living outside the Western world have neither the assurance of survival nor the hope of any identity. They bear a doubly miserable load in a world where, with increased communication, they are aware that more and more people can both survive and be recognized as human. In poor countries the appeal of gaining an identity, as much as the desire for survival, often makes many men blind followers of political demagogues who promise them a dependent role.

In our attempts to understand our behavior, we judge ourselves too much by the recent past. We have ignored a need built into us for four million years. Even the entire 10,000 years of the survival society is not enough time to destroy our genetic need for involvement and to evolve a new need for hostile, suspicious, competitive antagonism that was often useful in survival society.

Some people think that because, from Carthage to My Lai, man has demonstrated inhumanity to his fellow man, he has an inherent desire to harm other men. These instances occurred, however, when man was forced by his need for survival, or what he believed to be so, to suppress his need for involvement. Hostile, destructive, competitive behavior is not natural; it is not built in. Man is potentially more akin to what he was during the 500,000 years that preceded civilization than what he has forced himself to be during the moment of time called history.

Sometimes it is claimed that the world has known civilized societies in which identity, not survival, was the basic motivation. One example commonly cited is ancient Greece. Greece, however, and all previous large civilizations that "valued" humanity were built on slavery or a low servile class. It may have been an identity society for Plato but not for the slaves who created the security that allowed him to develop his identity.

As I have said, the primitive identity societies first ended when destruction of game caused them to turn toward agriculture. No longer could the availability of land be taken for granted. In the struggle to acquire and hold property, those who were stronger, smarter, or luckier did better; those who were weaker, dumber, or unlucky struggled for survival under the domination of others. Civilization is characterized by the organization of groups that exercise control and power for self-protection and aggrandizement. When any group, small or large, becomes strong enough so that others do not prey on it and satisfied enough so that it does not prey on others and waste itself in conflict, it may then start to concern itself with identity, with human rights and privileges; the United States, Canada, Switzerland, and Sweden are examples of countries in which some degree of this concern has been present for a long time.

Despite some concern for identity, survival societies are power hierarchies. The top is occupied by a few powerful people, the bottom by large masses grubbing for existence at a bare survival level. Between the two is a wide variety of people who make up the middle classes of any civilization. Power keeps these classes in their established order. One moves up if he gains power, down if he loses power. Any upward movement within the society threatens others because there are limited places to go. If too many or too few people exist within a class, their survival is threatened; there is either not enough or too much work for them to do. Conflict occurs when they try either to move out or to keep others from moving in.

Power is jealously guarded. People at all levels are aware that the social structure is fragile; if too many people try to move up, there is conflict above and below. As its members fight to move up, a social class is weakened, giving others the chance to move up themselves. However many classes exist, it is always the large bottom group, the slaves, serfs, peasants, or millhands, who do the hard, disagreeable work for the society. If many of them stop working, the whole hierarchy is threatened; any attempt to organize this class and give it power is therefore strenuously resisted, not only by those at the top but by almost everyone above the bottom.

India, with its rigid caste system, was a classic survival society. Had the lower-caste people refused to do the basic work, the whole society would have starved. Ancient Egypt, Greece, Rome, and the antebellum South of the United States were societies built on slaves, the lowest possible rung in the hierarchy. Serfs, peasants, fellahs, and factory workers and miners, adult and child, provided the base for wealth and luxury at the top during past centuries. Those with power always kept the workers close to bare survival; if the worker stopped he starved. Some people did go hungry—hunger was a reality to be feared, not an idle threat.

Many people with no identity tried to gain a little security and a dependent role within the power structure by taking on aspects of their ruler's identity. History is replete with people who followed blindly, often to their own destruction, a leader who gave them identity. Nazi Germany is an example: after World War I rich and powerful people, stung by defeat and loss of prestige, persuaded both the upward-aspiring middle classes and the always desperate lower classes to chase an illusion of power that destroyed thirty million people.

A power hierarchy, led sometimes by charismatic leaders but always by strong leaders, began and continues to rule every civilized society. Powerful societies developed and came increasingly into conflict as they competed for land and resources. To increase their power these societies developed sophisticated technologies for destruction and waged war frequently (about this history is quite factual). They were seldom deterred by huge losses of human life. Because most human beings, especially those who did the fighting, were worth so little and had so little power, waging war was never effectively challenged by any group within the survival society. War, the organized and systematic killing of one's fellow man, became a way of life throughout the history of civilized societies.

Organization for war, especially in highly technical societies, can become a national goal to which the whole society subscribes. Soldiers who fight the war, politicians who direct the war, and workers who supply the needs of the war all gain a strong, well-defined subordinate or *dependent role.* In a limited way, war provides a role for many people who have no role; in the beginning or when they are winning they welcome this chance. An individual, soldier or civilian, gains a role only to the extent that he reinforces the goal of winning the war. War, which started from the conflict for survival, has developed far in excess of its original purpose; it has taken on an identity of its own. Of course some wars, ancient and modern, were fought for survival, at least by one side; World War II is a recent example. Many wars, however, have been fought in which neither side could make a reasonable claim that the war increased its chance of survival. These wars were fought exclusively for power; World War I, that classic of senseless wars, best illustrates this situation.

In a survival society, attaining an independent role or a human identity is impossible for most people and difficult for the remaining few. The only identity possible for almost everyone in such a society is an identity narrowly related to work or class—a dependent role. The role depends on what one does rather than who one is. Sometimes a period of peace and prosperity provides substantial security for certain people. A person who becomes secure enough to be unconcerned about the power of leaders and the need to work for survival can respond to his innate need for involvement and learn to relate to people in a nonpower, human way. He can do so to feel good, not to assure his place in the power structure.

When people experience satisfaction of their need for involvement, an independent or a mostly independent role becomes possible. This independent role is potentially about the same for everyone; we gain a successful identity as a human being separate from what we do. Enjoying ourselves as people, we help others do the same. We can give free vent to what we feel and what we wish to do as long as we do not deprive others of the same choice. We feel successful, wanted, and valuable as a person. We are living through a time in which about a half billion people at all levels of the power structure have enough security to make a role-dominated identity society again become a reality. After 10,000 years of power-dominated, goal-oriented civilization, most of us in the Western world are rapidly moving into a new civilized identity society. It is both the occurrence and the characteristics of this *civilized identity society* that are the thrust of this book starting in Chapter One.

Index

Sensitivity training, 43
Separation, 39–40
Settlement houses, 43
Sexual behavior
 and children, 121, 164–170
 and commitment, 184, 185–186
 double standards, 176, 179–180
 and failure, 164–165
 gratification, 24
 and guilt, 175–176
 without involvement, 181–182
 and loneliness, 181, 182, 183
 and long-term affairs, 185–186
 and marriage, 178
 and pleasure, 31, 32, 33, 238
 and sadism, 67
 and single standard, 184–185
 and women's initiative, 186–187
Shock treatments, 51
Singles groups, 43
Sirhan Sirhan, 217
Siskin, Prof. B., 231–232
Slave societies, 245
Smoking, 54, 151
 and children, 118
Social discord, 108
Socialization
 infant, 104–105
 and television, 106–107
Societal identity, 72–73
Society
 defying, 92–93
 and protective imprisonment, 197–198
Soldiers, behavior of, 232–233
Solitary confinement, 31
South, United States, antebellum, 245
Speed, 157. *See also* Amphetamines
Stalin, 68
Stomachache, 47
Stress, 29, 36
Styles, attention-getting, 67
Success, 35, 36
Successful behavior, 28–29

Suicide, 56
Survival and pain, 26–27
Survival society, 233, 234, 236–237
Suspicion and loneliness, 31
Sweden, 244
Swindling, 66
Switzerland, 244
Symptoms
 chosen, 56–58, 61
 development, 56
 secondary, 61
Synanon, 42, 54–55, 151, 162, 163, 200, 219, 224

Tea and Sympathy (Anderson), 181
Tehachapi, 196 *n.*
Television
 and children, 106–107
 influence of, 14
 and involvement, 20
 and security, 21–22
Tension, 28
Terkel, Studs, 4
Territorial expansion, 240–241
Therapists
 and excuses, 96–99
 personality, 78–83
 and planning, 93–99
 and punishment, 99–102
 reality, 74–75
Therapy for children, 170–173
Thrill-seeking, 67–68
Tranquilizers, 42
Trial, criminal, 201, 202, 204–205
Turnbull, C., 232

Ulcers, 61, 62
Unreality and loneliness, 31
Uppers. *See* Amphetamines

Valium, 155
Value judgments, 90–91
 and children, 110
 and commitments, 96–97

About the Author

At present William Glasser works extensively both in psychiatry, where he continues to develop the ideas of Reality Therapy, and in education, where his ideas, published in his 1969 book *Schools Without Failure,* are widely used throughout the United States and Canada. He heads an organization, the Educator Training Center, which in affiliation with La Verne College has over 25,000 teachers actively involved in studying and working to make their school a school without failure. Many more teachers are involved in his courses on educational television. Psychiatric clinics, mental hospitals, halfway houses, and correctional institutions are now using the ideas of Reality Therapy. At the Institute of Reality Therapy in West Los Angeles he teaches and consults with those interested in learning to use Reality Therapy in their work and in their lives.